the Story of Eve

the STORY of EVE

selected poems

حوّا کی کہانی

ZEHRA NIGAH

Translated by

RAKHSHANDA JALIL

SPEAKING TIGER BOOKS
125A, Ground Floor, Shahpur Jat
New Delhi – 110049

First published by Speaking Tiger Books, 2024

ISBN: 978-93-5447-721-8
eISBN: 978-93-5447-720-1

10 9 8 7 6 5 4 3 2 1

This book is dedicated to Mrs Indira Varma, who introduced me to Zehra Aapa long years ago and has been an abiding friend to both of us through good times and bad.

Portrait of Zehra Nigah by M.F. Husain
(Courtesy Zehra Nigah.)

CONTENTS

INTRODUCTION

One of the first women to gain recognition and fame in the almost entirely male-dominated field of Urdu poetry, Zehra Nigah is today counted among the greatest living Urdu poets. In a career spanning over six decades, she has written nazms and ghazals that are as personal as they are political, but always intimate and deeply felt, and composed in the tradition of classical Urdu poetry.

Besides her writing, she has also earned great acclaim for her renditions at *mushairas* in South Asia and beyond, where she has been a much loved and eagerly awaited figure for decades. Amidst friends and family, she is equally well known as a raconteur par excellence and a *qissa-go,* a teller of engaging tales. Zehra Aapa, as she is affectionately known, talks as she writes: with grace and poise and wry humour and is, therefore, a delightful conversationalist.

Zehra Nigah was born in 1936 in Hyderabad, India, and migrated to Karachi, Pakistan with her family in 1947. She began to recite her poetry at *mushairas* from a fairly young age, which was considered unusual at the time, especially so for a young woman from a *shareef,* 'respectable', Muslim family.

As one of very few women Urdu poets to gain prominence at the time, she was a pioneer, but she has refused to wear the label of a 'woman poet'. She has always deplored labels and has insisted that she views the world around her through the eyes of a woman, yes, but her concerns are not those of a woman alone.

Treading the fine line between feminism and 'feminine' verse, she has steadfastly refused to allow gender to dictate her choice of subjects. Her poetry is as much about the compulsions and compromises of being a woman and a poet, as it is about a sensitive, thinking person's response to all that is happening in the world around her. To her, the 'sorrow of the world' is as important, if not more, as the 'sorrow of the heart'.

Despite early critical and popular acclaim, Zehra Nigah has not published much. In the course of a conversation during one of her frequent visits to Delhi, she made a very interesting observation to me. She pointed out how the *majmua-e-kalam* (collected works) of even some of the greatest poets have a lot of padding or fluff; she used a delightfully colloquial expression: '*bharti ke sher*', alluding to the unevenness that is regarded as inevitable and therefore taken as a matter of course in the *diwan*, or complete works, of even the best of poets, be they Mir or Firaq. It is a rare poet, she said, who exercises enormous self-restraint and is capable of a rigorous self-edit to publish a collection of his or her poetry that is free of any form of excess. Faiz Ahmad Faiz, according to her, was one such poet. So was Ghalib, who was ruthless about what he wanted to excise from the *diwan* that was published in his lifetime. To my mind, Zehra Aapa is another such poet. She has published only four slim collections—*Shaam ka Pehla Taara* ('The First Star of the Evening'), *Warq* ('Page'), *Firaq* ('Separation') and, most recently, *Gul Chandni* (a white fragrant flower of the Gardenia family that blooms at night and is similar to Jasmine)—and not one has a *'bharti ka sher'*.

Slender though they are, all four collections contain veritable gems and plucking and choosing from those gems for this selection was a delightfully difficult task.*

***

Always immaculately dressed in impeccable cotton saris, given to no adornments except the smile she chooses to bestow occasionally, Zehra Aapa is a woman completely at peace with herself. But as she says in the much-recited, much-quoted nazm *'Samjhauta'* ('Compromise'), the easy calm hides the many compromises that she—like all women—has had to make:

Warm and soft, this blanket of compromise,
It has taken me years to weave it.
No flowers of truth embellish it
Not a stitch of falsehood betrays it.

It will do to cover my body,
And it will keep you satisfied, although
It will bring you neither joy nor sadness.

Is she a writer of feminine poetry or a feminist poet? I asked her once, many years ago, in the course of a formal interview for a newspaper. She replied that she dislikes compartmentalization of any kind. It is human

---

*Recently her collected works have been published in Urdu by the Anjuman Tarrqui-e Urdu—Hind in India and all of her poetry is now available between the covers of one volume.

experience that she writes about, and as a human being. But her identity as a woman is significant. She speaks in a woman's tongue, using a feminine idiom and images to make powerful social and political comments. In lyrical, pathos-driven yet politically astute poems such as *'Bhejo Nabi ji Rehmatein'* and *'Qissa Gul Badshah'*, she has alluded to the bitter fratricidal war that culminated in the creation of Bangladesh, as well as the heart-rending situation in Afghanistan and, more recently, the surgical strikes through remote-controlled drones by the US army. She has written of the repressive Hudood Ordinances introduced during General Zia's oppressive regime, as also about love, friendship and small everyday joys and sorrows. A poem about female foeticide, *'Mai Bach Gayii Ma'*, was occasioned by the brutal statistics on the sheer numbers of missing girl children:

I was saved, Mother, I was saved,
The henna of your unripe blood has seeped into every pore of my being.

Had my features formed, they too would have filled with blood.
Had my eyes learnt to see, they would have been rimmed with the kohl of acid.
[...]
Every dream I dreamt would have remained unfulfilled.
Had I gained a little height, my father would have lost a few inches,
Had my veil slipped from my head, my brother's turban would have fallen.
Mother, before I could hear your lullaby, I've slipped into a sleep of my own.

When I asked her how the language, imagery and structure of her poems evolve, Zehra Aapa said that just about anything can 'trigger the creative process'—a news report, a scene on a road, a sudden memory, a fragrance, a painting. A newspaper headline about the rape of countless women by marauding West Pakistani forces in East Pakistan (now Bangladesh) in 1971 resulted in the chilling poem *'Bhejo Nabi ji Rehmatein'*. The subject of the poem is brutality, the atrocities and sexual crimes perpetrated by men on women during a war, yet it employs everyday images of tranquil domesticity—a woman teaching her pet parrot to invoke the Prophet's blessings, the chapati on the *tawa,* the pot bubbling on the hearth, the infant rocking in its cradle. The seeming gentleness of the opening and the sudden violence makes the poem far more powerful and shattering than any reportage. The effect is stronger because nowhere does it contain any direct reference to the actual political context; it is left to us as readers to infer the sub-text—and even as we do, the realization becomes inescapable that this could happen anywhere, at any time, in any war, riot or conflict.

Similarly, a TV report on the use of landmines in Afghanistan resulted in the song-like *'Qissa Gul Badshah'* featuring a child soldier in a war that the adults around him have long ceased to comprehend. A war that has maimed and mutilated countless boys too young to understand the 'cause' that they are fighting for; a cause for which they are forced to bear arms:

People say this is a War of Peace
And in a War of Peace the attackers

Only leave the children without hands and feet,
They don't leave them hungry;
After all, there is such a thing as humanity.

Alone in these smouldering mountains
I stand holding the gun I have inherited as my legacy.
I used to watch the spectacle of those granting favours;
I still watch the spectacle of those granting favours.

***

When Zehra Nigah began to make a mark as a poet in the 1950s and 60s, women poets were a rarity. Women from respectable families were not encouraged to come on stage to recite their poetry, let alone express themselves with any degree of intimacy and independence. So, she hid her convictions, her independent spirit and moral courage behind a quiet, 'feminine' persona, a demureness; she read her poems at *mushairas* with eyes downcast and scuttled back to the safe haven of domesticity. But before long, the sheer lyricism of her words, the engaging simplicity of her poetic idiom and the sharp insightful comments couched therein—not to mention the felicity of her *tarannum* (a stylized, melodious manner of reciting poetry)—built her a formidable reputation and earned her a legion of admirers. To this day, a hush invariably descends at noisy *mushairas* when she stands up to recite her poetry, though with advancing age she politely declines requests to recite in *tarannum,* preferring to read her poetry *tahtul-lafz,* a sonorous way of reading poetry so that every word, every syllable, every phrase comes alive and the listener draws fully of both the felicity of words and expressions as well as the depth of meaning. Every word that emerges from her pen, every syllable that she speaks, carries the spark of a luminous intelligence.

Zehra Aapa has never felt the urge to be prolific, to write when there is nothing to say. Her poetry holds a clue to another possible reason:

Zehra has not written anything at all for many days,
Although there's much she has seen in this time.
If she were to write, what can she write?
And what can she think?
Her thoughts are a bit ambiguous, her hands shake somewhat.

Zehra has not written anything at all for many days.
She's not so foolish that she will spit out whatever is on her tongue.
It isn't lightly that she has taken this fast of silence,
Nor is she so old that she will tire easily.
This manner, it's a deliberate choice.
She has put away everything in the Trunk of Forgetfulness,
It is a good way to live life easily, simply.

Another reason, perhaps, is that she is a classicist, not in the content of her verse but in style. Her distinctive verse, seemingly simple yet syntactically complex, adheres to an older poetic diction. Here is just one example:

Ruk ja hujoom-e-gul keabhihauslanahin
Dil se ḳhayaal-e-tangi-e-daamaangayanahin

(Stop! O crowd of flowers, for I don't have the courage yet,
The thought of my meagre means still lingers in my heart.)

This might be a good place to talk briefly about Zehra Aapa's ghazals. But first, a short digression about exactly what is the ghazal and how it differs from the nazm might be in order.

An Arabic word meaning an 'amatory ode' or 'talking to women', the ghazal's primary subject has all along been romantic love. Coming to Urdu in a virtually unbroken tradition from Arabic through Persian, the ghazal flowered dramatically in 18th-century India in the hands of poets such as Mir and Sauda. Across a vast expanse from Delhi to the Deccan, Urdu poets made the ghazal a thing of rare and exquisite beauty, glittering like burnished gold and capable of saying the most profound things in the fewest possible words.

A ghazal comprises several two-line couplets. The two lines, each called a *misra* which together constitute a *sher,* are considered enough in themselves to complete a thought, a thought that may or may not be picked up or echoed in subsequent verses of the same ghazal. The first *sher* is called a *matla,* and the last *sher* is called a *maqta* which more often than not contains the pen name or *takhallus* of the poet*; there should be a minimum of five *sher* in a *ghazal.* Then there's the *radeef* and *qafiya,* two prerequisites for a poetic composition to be deemed a ghazal. The *qafiya* is the rhyming pattern of words that must directly precede the ghazal's *radeef* (repeated words), usually following a rhyme scheme of *aa, ba, ca, da,* and so on.

The fixed prosody and structure of the ghazal demands great exactitude from the poet; at the same time, contrary though it may sound, this very fixedness allows a lazy poet to get away merely with stringing together the right

*Zehra Aapa does not use a takhallus, though she often refers to herself by her name in her nazms as in '*Zehra ne bahut din se kuchh bhi nahi likha hai*' ('Zehra has not written anything at all for many days').

words in the right sequence and managing to make an impact both visually (through word images) or aurally (through the intrinsic musicality of the chosen word combinations). Often when one reads a *sher* carefully or gets past the enchantment of the words, one finds the *sher* to be a chimera, amounting to nothing more than stardust.

Unlike a ghazal, which can sometimes get away with just sounding beautiful but meaning very little, or at best presenting no startling new idea or thought, the nazm (meaning simply verse but used in Urdu poetry to distinguish a form of verse that is *not* a ghazal) absolutely must say something to justify its existence. A nazm is read, while a ghazal is always recited, because of its inherent musicality.*

In the early days, when Zehra Aapa used to recite her poetry at *mushairas*, it was mostly her ghazals that established her reputation as a poet. However, with time and the evolution of her voice as a poet, she increasingly came to be known for her nazms and her distinctive style of reciting them. This could possibly be because the nazm lends itself more naturally, more organically to a host of social and political issues. This is not to say that the ghazal is not, or cannot, be a vehicle for political expression; Faiz Ahmad Faiz and Ahmad Faraz

---

*It must be stressed that the purpose of this digression is not to pit the one against the other and stress the superiority, or inferiority, of the nazm or the ghazal. It seemed, to me, the simplest way to delineate the basic differences between the two for the uninitiated reader. It must also be stressed that these are broad, general points of difference and not actual markers for any one poet or his/her work, least of all Zehra Aapa's.

have written intensely political poetry in the time-honoured format of the ghazal. But there is an energy, a momentum, a directness that the nazm has which allows a freer, sharper, more pointed way of making an overt statement.*

All selected works are by their very definition subjective, and in this collection I too am guilty of a certain partisanship. Of the total 76 poems selected here for translation, 65 are nazms and only 11 are ghazals. These numbers reflect my own preference for 'poetry of substance' and immediate, contemporary relevance. Also, and this needs to be said, the nazm lends itself more easily and more felicitously to translation; the Urdu ghazal, with its haiku-like brevity and compactness, its constraints and rhyme scheme is more stubbornly resistant to translation across the picket fences of languages, especially languages as disparate as Urdu and English, both with their distinct word patterns, sounds and syntax, not to mention the natural silences between words.

Having said that, I am struck by an occasional *nazm-numa* (nazm-like) quality in Zehra Aapa's ghazals, such as here:

Eik ke ghar ki ḳhidmat ki aur eik se dil se mohabbat ki
Donon farz nibha kar uss ne saari umr ibadat ki

(She served in the house of one, and loved the other with all her heart
She fulfilled both her duties and spent all her life in prayer)

*I have dwelt at great length on the *ghazal* and the *nazm*, the differences between the two and how modern poets have used them towards different ends in my book *Shahryar: A Life in Poetry* (Harper Collins, 2018)

Nazm or ghazal, Zehra Aapa excels in getting to the heart of the matter almost without effort, but with maximum impact. Commentators such as Ahmad Nadeem Qasmi, the respected Urdu writer, have noted Zehra Aapa's unique *lahja* (tone and tenor). Writing the Foreword to her collection *'Warq'*, Qasmi sahab pointed out the *dheemaapan* (moderation, mildness or subtlety) of her poetic voice, her ability to say 'big' things in a seemingly conversational, easy manner:

> 'The discerning readers had gauged from Zehra Nigah's earliest work that an entire universe of possibilities is contained within her poetry...she kept treading with a slow and steady pace the Highway of Evolution... [She] takes up the gravest and most sombre subjects with such ease as though she is talking of events and happenings that are taking place right in front of her. Those who know Zehra, those who know the mildness and moderation of her voice and the genteel, polite, courteous, civilized persona that is amply in evidence, are surprised that she is able to present the most hideous, the most dreadful scenarios in the most subtle manner. Some of the most terrible situations have been rendered by her pen through such eloquent and articulate symbols and suggestions that her reader or listener can feel the high waves of pain crash into their hearts.
>
> Zehra has the utmost respect for relationships, rapports, friendships; she feels the pain most keenly when they break or are defeated, or decline amidst chaos and confusion. While she may be breaking up from inside, the gusts of disappointment and disillusionment never snuff out the flame of hope and faith. If anything, she uses that slough of darkness and

despondency to give birth to a new dawn. For several reasons, Zehra's new collection, *Warq*, will prove to be a...benchmark in the history of Urdu poetry.'

***

Apart from the poetry for which she is justly well known, Zehra Aapa has also written scripts for TV drama serials and films. Two of her siblings have been associated with the television industry: her older sister Fatima Suraiyya Bajia was a much-acclaimed scriptwriter and her brother Anwar Maqsood is a famous writer, satirist and television host. Today, she spends time in her home in Karachi which is filled with books and paintings, or travels to stay with her son and her extended family in different parts of the world. But whether she is at home or abroad, books and reading remain an essential part of her life. As she writes in her poem '*Virsa*' ('Legacy'):

I'm looking back to see
All that I received as legacy
And all that I'm leaving behind.

My home was wrecked by storms,
My ancestors had seen
The demon of the age
That snatched everything from them.
And yet there was much that I received:
There was the lustre of hard work on their faces
There was the gleam of self-respect in their eyes.
Their hands rested on each other, yet
How full were those hands!
And the habit of living together amicably—

All this I had received from that home
The home that was an empty house.

In my own large family
In my happy home
I have bequeathed fear
I have broken the bonds of courage.

There is an economy of words in what is said
And such dread in nearness,
Everyone with their own joys, their separate spaces
Their own toys, their own being

I'm looking back to see…

Rakhshanda Jalil
October 2024
New Delhi

I
Nazm

Havva ki Kahani

Tumhein seb khaane ki tarqeeb maine nahiin dii
Vo gehoon ka daana meri dastaras mein nahi thha
Meri saanp se dosti bhi nahiin thhi

Agar dosti thhi kisi se, vo tum thhe
Agar koi achha laga thha, vo tum thhe

The Story of Eve

I did not compel you to eat the apple
Nor was that grain of wheat grown on my palm,
And the serpent—he was no friend of mine.

If I had a friend, it was you.
If I loved someone, it was you.

Bhejo Nabi ji Rehmatein

Eik ghar thha, eik maidaan thha
Kuchh khet thhe, khalihaan thha
Chalti sadak bhi saath thhi
Vo ghar mein tanha to naa thhi
Handi thhi chulhe par charhi
Aanta gundha tayyar thha

Jhoole mein ik bachcha bhi thha
Pinjare mein ik tota bhi thha
Aur taaq par Quran thha
Jis par usse imaan thha
Chulhe ko sulgaati thhi vo
Bachche ko behlaati thhi vo
Tote ko sikhlati thhi vo
Achche Miyan Mitthu kaho:
'Bhejo Nabi ji barkatein
Bhejo Nabi ji rehmatein
Aal-e-Nabi ka vaasta
Aal-e-Nabi ka vaasta!'

Eik din achanak kya hua
Thokar se darwaza khula
Ik jaanwar insan-numa
Panjon ko lehraata huwa
Kamre mein aata hii gaya
Har sheh pe chhaata hii gaya

Send Mercies Upon Us, O Prophet Ji

There was a home, an open ground,
Some fields and farmlands
And a busy road.
She was not alone in her home.
The pot was bubbling on the hearth,
The dough was kneaded and ready.

There was a baby in a hammock, too.
And a parrot in a cage
And the Quran in a niche,
The Quran in which she had complete faith.
She would coo to her baby,
She would blow into her stove,
She would teach her parrot:
My dear Mr Parrot, say:
'Send mercies upon us, O Prophet ji.
Send mercies upon us, O Prophet ji,
I beseech you in the name of your kin,
I beseech you in the name of your kin!'

One day, suddenly,
Someone kicked the door open
And an animal-like human
Waving its claw-like hands
Entered the room
And kept coming all the way in
Darkening everything in its shadow

Chaadar jo sar se khinch gayi
Quran ka chehra dhak gaya
Roti tawe par jal gayi
Handi ubal kar rah gayi
Bachche ka jhoola gir parha
Tota pharhak kar cheekh utha:
'Bhejo Nabi ji barkatein
Bhejo Nabi ji rehmatein
Aal-e-Nabi ka vaasta
Aal-e-Nabi ka vaasta!'

Par koi aaya hii nahin

The veil was ripped off her head
The face of the Quran was covered
The roti burnt on the *tawa*
The pot on the fire boiled over
The baby fell from the hammock
The parrot cried out in agony—
'Send mercies upon us O Prophet ji
Send mercies upon us O Prophet ji
I beseech you in the name of your kin
I beseech you in the name of your kin!'

But no one came.

Samjhauta

Mulayam garm samjhaute ki chaadar
Ye chaadar main ne barson mein buni hai
Kahin bhi sach ke gul-boote nahin hain
Kisi bhi jhooth ka taanka nahin hai

Issi se main bhi tan dhak loongi apna
Issi se tum bhi aasooda rahoge
Na ḳhush hoge na pazhmurda rahoge

Issi ko taan kar ban jaega ghar
Bichha leinge to khil utthega aangan
Utha lenge to gir jaegi chilman

Compromise

Warm and soft, this blanket of compromise,
It has taken me years to weave it.
No flowers of truth embellish it
Not a stitch of falsehood betrays it.

It will do to cover my body,
And it will keep you satisfied, although
It will bring you neither joy nor sadness.

Stretched overhead, it will make us a home.
Spread beneath us, it will brighten up our courtyard.
When we drop it, the screen* will fall.

---

*The original word, chilman, refers to the reed-curtain that screened the women's quarter in homes and institutions. It was a kind of collective purdah.

Main Bach Gai Ma, Main Bach Gai

Main bach gai ma
Main bach gai ma
Tire kachche lahu ki mehndi
Mire por por mein rach gai ma
Main bach gai ma
Gar mere naqsh ubhar aate
Vo phir bhi lahu se bhar jaate
Miri ankhein raushan ho jaati to
Tezaab ka surma lag jaata
Satte-vatte mein bat jaati
Be-kaari mein kaam aa jaati
Har ḳhwaab adhoora rah jaata
Mira qad jo thoda sa badhta
Mire baap ka qad chhota padta
Miri chunari sar se dhalak jaati
Mire bhai ki pagdi gir jaati
Tiri lori sunne se pahle
Apni niind mein so gai ma
Anjaan nagar se aai thhi
Anjaan nagar mein kho gai ma
Main bach gai ma
Main bach gai ma

I was Saved, Mother, I was Saved

I was saved, Mother, I was saved,
The henna of your unripe blood has seeped
    into every pore of my being.

Had my features formed, they too would have
    filled with blood.
Had my eyes learnt to see, they would have been
    rimmed with the kohl of acid.
I would have been bartered in *satta-vatta** or used up in *kari*†.
Every dream I dreamt would have remained unfulfilled.
Had I gained a little height, my father would have
    lost a few inches,
Had my veil slipped from my head, my brother's turban
        would have fallen.
Mother, before I could hear your lullaby, I've slipped
        into a sleep of my own.
I came from a strange land; I have gone away to a strange land.

I was saved, Mother, I was saved,
The henna of your unripe blood has seeped
        into every pore of my being.

---

*Refers to a type of 'exchange marriage' where two sets of siblings marry each other. In order to get married, a man needs to persuade his sister to marry the bride's brother.

†The practice of honour killing

Suna Hai

Suna hai jangalon ka bhi koi dastoor hota hai
Suna hai sher ka jab pet bhar jaae to vo hamla nahin karta
Daraḳhton ki ghani chhanv mein jaa kar let jaata hai
Hawa ke tez jhonke jab daraḳhton ko hilaate hain
To maina apne bachche chhod kar
Kavve ke andon ko paron se thhaam leti hai
Suna hai ghonsle se koi bachcha gir pade to saara jangal
    jaag jaata hai
Suna hai jab kisi naddi ke paani mein
Bae ke ghonsle ka gandumi rang larazta hai
To naddi ki rupahli machhliyan uss ko padosan maan leti hain
Kabhi toofan aa jaae, koi pul tuut jaae to
Kisi lakdi ke taḳhte par
Gilahri, sanp, bakri aur cheeta saath hote hain
Suna hai jangalon ka bhi koi dastoor hota hai
Khudavanda! Jaleel-o-Mo'tabar! Daana-o-Biina Munsif-o-Akbar!
Mire iss shahr mein ab jangalon hii ka koi qanoon nafiz kar!
Koi dastoor nafiz kar!

I Have Heard

I've heard that even jungles have their rules.
I've heard that when a lion's belly is full, he does not kill,
He goes to lie down in the dense shade of trees.
When strong gusts of wind shake the trees,
The myna leaves her own fledglings
And protects the crow's eggs under her wings.
I've heard that if a little bird falls from its nest, the entire jungle comes to life.
I've heard that when the wheat-coloured nest of a tailorbird
Quivers in the waters of a river,
The silvery fish see it as their neighbour.
When a storm comes, when a bridge breaks,
Squirrel, snake, goat and cheetah are to be found
Together on some plank of wood.
Dear Lord! O Glorious and Revered One! O Wise, All-seeing Greatest of Judges!
Issue the laws of the jungle in this city of mine!
Issue some rules!

Yahaan Dildar Begum Dafn Hain

Eik anjana sa dar
Jab vo paida hui thhi
Uss ke andar jazb thha

Eik andheri kothari ka ḳhauf
Rag rag mein basa thha
Eik unchai se gir jaane ki dahshat
Peechhe peechhe chal rahi thhi
Eik darwaaze ke peechhe ja ke chhup jaane ka shauq
Zindagi ki sab se pahli aarzu thhi
Khidkiyon ki ote se galiyon ka manzar dekhna
Zindagi ki sab se pahli justuju thhi

Jab zara sa waqt guzra
Aql ke taaron ki jumbish se badan jaaga
Hifazat ka tasavvur iss qadar wahshat-zada thha
Ki apne jism se sharmindagi hoti rahi

Phir ḳharidaron ki duniya mein zara sun-gun hui
Dil dhadakne ki sada maaduum ho kar rah gai
Khauf ke gahne saja kar
Aur jhijak ke be-tahaasha phuul pahna kar
Kharidaron ne uss ko phir se andhi kothari mein qaid kar daala
Vo jis ka ḳhauf vo bachpan se sahti aa rahi thhi
Phir zara sa hosh aaya
Daur-e-nau-umri gaya to aankh se parda hata
Manzar nazar aane lagey
Paanv chaukhat ki taraf badhne lagey
Ik qadam rakkha hii thha ki nanhe nanhe haath ik
zanjir ban kar aa gaye

Dildar Begum is Buried Here

When she was born
Her being was already imbued
With an unknown fear.

The dread of a dark chamber
Was steeped in every pore.
The terror of falling from a great height
Dogged every footstep.
To hide herself behind the shelter of a door
Had been her earliest wish,
To watch the spectacle in the streets through shuttered windows
Had been her first desire.

As time passed,
The stirring of the chords of her brain awakened her body,
And then the spectre of safety grew so terrifying
That she became ashamed of her body.

Then murmurs arose in the community of buyers
And the sound of a beating heart was muffled.
Adorned with the ornaments of fear,
Weighed down with countless flowers of diffidence,
She was imprisoned again by the buyers in a dark chamber,
The same chamber that had terrified her since her childhood.

Some semblance of awareness came
As adolescence passed and the veils before her eyes parted
To reveal the spectacle of the world.
Her feet moved towards the threshold, then.
She had barely set one foot forward, when tiny hands reached out,
like manacles.

Ab vo iss raste mein hai sab jis ko rah-e-marg kahte hain
Munjamid ankhon mein ab manzar thhaharte hii nahin
Ab kisi chaukhat ki jaanib paanv badhte hii nahin
Nanhe nanhe haath kuchh iss tarah unche ho gaye
Ab dastaras se duur hain
Apni zanjiron mein ḳhud mahsur hain
Iss ki andhi kothari par ek katba nasb hai

'Is jagah Dildar Begum dafn hai
Vo afifa parsa sabir-o-shakir so rahi hai
Yahan se ġhair mardon ka guzarna mana hai
Baraae fatiha jo aana chahe aaye
Lekin duur se padh le'

Now she stands on a road that is said to be the path of death.
The spectacles of the world do not stay fixed in her glazed eyes.
Now her feet do not move towards any threshold.
The tiny hands have grown so big,
Her hands cannot reach or hold them.
Now she's a captive of her own chains.

This epitaph is affixed on her dark chamber:
'Dildar Begum is buried here.
That pure, pious, patient and praise-worthy woman
    sleeps here.
Unrelated men are forbidden to come close;
Those who wish to offer prayers
May do so from a distance.'

STOP

Thhehro keh kar jaise kisi ne waqt ka darya roke diya hai
Ek tilismi harf ke jis ki taaqat ka ab ilm hua hai
Apni apni simt mein behta har har lamha thahr gaya hai
Saare dost aur saare dushman patthar ban kar dekh rahein hain
Kaisi anhoni lagti hai?
Haalanke ye shehr-e-kharaabi jis din se taamiir huwa thha
Uss din se iss baat ka dar thha

STOP

It is as though someone has said, 'STOP',
    and halted the river of Time;
It is only now that I have fully understood
    the magical properties of this word.
Each moment, flowing in its own orderly row, has stopped.
All my friends and all my enemies gaze at me,
    as though turned to stone.
How strange it seems.
Even though, since the day this benighted city was built
I've been scared of precisely such a thing.

Insaaf

Main iss chhote se kamre mein
Azaad bhi huun aur qaid bhi huun
Iss kamre mein ik khidki hai
Jo chhat ke barabar unchi hai
Jab suraj doobne lagta hai
Kamre ki chhat se guzarta hai
Mutthi bhar kirnon ke zarre
Khidki se andar aate hain
Main iss raste par chalti huun
Aur apne ghar ho aati huun

Mira baap abhi tak mere liye
Jab shahr se vapas aata hai
Chaadar kanghi kaajal choodi
Jaane kya kya le aata hai
Mere donon bhai ab bhi
Masjid mein padhne jaate hain
Ahkam-e-ḳhudavandi saare
Padhte hain aur dohraate hain
Aapa mere hisse ki roti
Changir mein dhak kar rakhti hai
Aur subh sawere uth kar vo
Roti chidiyon ko deti hai

Justice*

In this small room
I am free, and also confined.
There is a window in this room,
A little window near the ceiling,
When the sun begins to sink,
It passes over the roof of my room
And a handful of motes of sunlight
Come in through the window.
I walk in their path
And go visit my home.

My father, returning from the city
Still buys all manner of things:
Chadar, comb, kajal, bangles.
Both my brothers still
Go to the mosque to study,
They read all the commands of God
And repeat them too.
My elder sister still cooks
And keeps my share of roti
Covered in the bread basket,
And when she gets up in the morning,
Feeds it to the birds.

---

*For the blind girl who was punished under the Hudood Ordinances passed during General Zia's regime to 'bring Pakistani law in conformity with the injunctions of Islam'. The girl, Safia, was raped by her employers, but while they were acquitted, she was imprisoned for 'fornication'. Her pregnancy was used as evidence against her.

Ma meri kuchh pagal sii hai
Ya patthar chunti rahti hai
Ya daana chugti chidiyon se
Kuchh batein karti rahti hai

Vo kahti hai jab ye chidiyan
Sab iss ki baat samajh lengi
Chonchon mein patthar bhar lengi
Panjon mein sang samo lengi
Phir vo toofan aa jaega
Jis se har mimbar har munsif
Paara-paara ho jaega
Mera insaf karega vo
Jo sab ka hakim-e-aala hai
Sab jis ki nazar mein yaksan hain
Jo munsif izzat waala hai

Main ma ko kaise samjhaun
Kya main koi Khaana-e Kaaba huun?

My mother seems touched by madness,
She either gathers stones
Or speaks to the birds pecking grain.

She says when all those birds
Understand what she's saying,
They will fill their beaks with stones,
They will fill their claws with stones,
And then such a storm shall break
That it will smash every pulpit
And every judge to smithereens.
Justice will be done unto me
By Him, the Mightiest of Judges,
In whose eyes all are equal;
The Judge who is the most honourable.

How shall I make my mother understand—
Am I the Kaaba, the holiest of holies?*

*This refers to the miraculous birds (known as '*ababeel*') mentioned in Surah Al-Fil of the Quran that protected the Kaaba in Mecca from the Aksumite elephant army by dropping small stones on the army as it approached.

Qissa Gul Badshah Ka

Naam mera hai Gul Badshah
Umr meri hai terah baras
Aur kahaani
Meri umr ki tarah se muntashir muntashir
Muḳhtasar muḳhtasar

Meri be-naam be-chehra maa
Be-dawa mar gai
Baap ne uss ko burqe mein dafna diya
Uss ko dar thha ki munkir-nakeer
Meri Amma ka chehra na dekhein
Vaise zinda thhi, jab bhi vo madfun thhi

Baap ka naam Zartaj Gul
Umr battis baras
Vo mujahid shahadat ka talib rah-e-haq ka musafir hua
Aur jaam-e-shahaadat bhi uss ne
Apne bhai ke hathon piya
Jo shumaali mujahid thha
Aur panj-waqta namaazi bhi thha
Mas.ala iss shahadat ka peicheeda hai
Iss ko behtar yahi hai yahin chhorh dein
Ab bahar-haal Baba to jannat mein hain
Uss ke haathon mein jaam-e-tuhoor
Uss ki baanhon mein hoor-o-qusoor
Meri taqdeer mein bam, dhamaake, dhuan
Pighalti hui ye zamin
Bikharta hua aasman
Bad-az-marg vo zinda hai
Zindagi mujh se sharminda hai

The Tale of Gul Badshah

My name is Gul Badshah,
I'm thirteen years old.
And my story
Like my age is disorderly, dispersed,
Short, succinct.

My nameless, faceless mother
Died untended, untreated.
My father buried her in her own burqa.
He was fearful that Munkir Nakiir*
Would see my mother's face.
In any case, even when she lived, she had been buried.

My father's name was Zartaj Gul,
Age thirty-two.
He was a warrior craving martyrdom,
    a traveller on the road to Truth,
And he drank from the goblet of martyrdom
From his brother's hands
Who was a warrior from the northern region,
One who prayed five times a day.
This matter of martyrdom is a complicated one,
It's best to drop it here.
Anyhow, my father is now in heaven,
Holding a cup of paradisal nectar
With many a houri and nymph in his arms.
And in my destiny, nothing but bombs, noise and smoke;
This molten earth,
This scattering sky.
He is alive even after death,
Whereas life is ashamed of me even as I live

---

*Angels who will visit the dead in the grave and question them on their deeds and misdeeds

2

Kal sar-e-shaam dushman ne aate hue
Bam ke hamrah barsa diye
Mujh pe kuchh peele thaile
Jin se mujh ko mile

Gol roti ke tukde
Ek makkhan ki tikiya
Ek sharbat ki botal
Murabbe ka dabba

Iss ke badle mein vo le gae
Mere bhai ka dast-e-mashaqqat
Jis mein mannat ka dora bandha thha
Meri chhoti bahan ka vo paanv
Jis se rang-e-hina phoot ta thha

Log kahte hain ye amn ki jang hai
Amn ki jang mein hamla-avar
Sirf bachchon ko be-dast-o-pa chhodte hain
Uun ko bhooka nahin chhodte
Aḳhir insaniyat bhi koi cheez hai

Main dahakte pahadon mein tanha
Apne tarke ki bandooq thaame khada huun
Tamasha-e-ahl-e-karam dekhta thha
Tamasha-e-ahl-e-karam dekhta huun

2

Yesterday, as night fell, the enemy
Dropped some yellow packets—
Just as they'd dropped bombs.
In them I found
Pieces of round bread,
A slab of butter,
A bottle of sherbet,
A jar of jam.

In place of these they took away
My brother's strong hand
With the thread of a *mannat* still tied around it,
My younger sister's foot
Still aglow with the colour of henna.

People say this is a War of Peace
And in a War of Peace the attackers
Only leave the children without hands and feet,
They don't leave them hungry;
After all, there is such a thing as humanity.

Alone in these smouldering mountains
I stand holding the gun I have inherited as my legacy.
I used to watch the spectacle of those granting favours;
I still watch the spectacle of those granting favours.

Tan-e-Nahiif Se Amboh-e-Jabr Haar Gaya

Ab aansuon ke dhundalkon mein raushni dekho
Hujoom-e-marg se aawaz-e-zindagi ko suno
Suno ki tishna-dahan maalik-e-sabeel hue
Suno ki ḳhaak-basar waaris-e-faseel hue
Rida-e-chaak ne dastaar-e-shah ko taar kiya
Tan-e-nahiif se amboh-e-jabr haar gaya
Suno ki hirs-o-hawas qahr-o-zahr ka rela
Ghubaar-o-ḳhaar o ḳhash-o-ḳhaak hii ne thaam liya
Siyahiyan hii muqaddar hon jin nigaahon ka
Khuda bachaae unn aankhon ki shola-baari se
Daro ki zard-ruḳhaan neem-jan-o ḳhasta-tanaan
Hazaar baar mare aur laakh baar jiye
Vo log jin ko mayassar na aaye marham-e-waqt
Vo log talḳhii-e-taqdeer baant lete hain
Vo haath jin pe ho nafrat ka zang sadiyon se
Vo haath lohe ki deewar kaat dete hain

A Multitude of Tyrannies Have Been Defeated by the Frail of Body*

Look at the light in the fog of tears,
Listen to the voice of Life in the crowded Babel of Death.
Listen, the parched of throat have set up water stalls for the thirsty.
Listen, those who lived in dust now own the city's ramparts,
The torn cloak has put to shame the sash tied around kingly turbans,
A multitude of tyrannies have been defeated by the frail of body.
Listen, the rabble of lust and envy, of wrath and poison
Was stemmed by dust and thorn, by twigs and leaves;
God alone can save you from the fire-flames of those eyes
Whose glances are destined only for darkness.
Be warned: the pale-faced, half-dead, frail of body
Are killed a thousand times and brought to life a million times.
Those who cannot avail the balm of Time, they
Divide the bitterness of Fate among themselves.
Hands that have carried the rust of hatred for centuries
Can slice through the wall of iron.

*Written on 25 March 1971, when war clouds were gathering over the sub-continent and civil strife was gathering momentum in East Pakistan.

Ant

Daal deta thha koi daana mere raaste par
Anginat sham-o-sehra reing ke main jeeti thhi
Na-tawaan jism pe do daane utha laati thhi
Reingte reingte phir bil mein chali jaati thhi
Ek din dhoop ne ehsaas dilaya thha mujhe
Tu jo himmat karey inn pairon mein dum aa jaaye
Phir hawaon ne bhi ruk-ruk kar ye sargoshi ki
Bil ke baahar to nikal dekh zara duniya bhi
Main kharhe hone ki koshish mein bahut ghabraayi
Larhkharha kar main giri gir ke uthi chakraayi
Ain uss waqt koi aaya sahaare ke liye
Pehle seena mera mitti se laga rehta thha
Ab mera sar kisi shaane se tika rehta hai

Ant

Someone would fling a morsel before me:
That is how I crawled through life for
    countless mornings and evenings.
I would carry those morsels on my frail body
And, creeping and crawling, return to my hole.
Till one day the sun made me realize:
If you want, you can bring strength to these legs.
And the winds too stopped to whisper:
Come out of your hole, look at the world!
I was afraid of standing on my own.
I tottered and fell, got up and swayed unsteadily,
Till, suddenly, someone came to steady me.
My chest used to hug the ground;
Now my head rests against someone's shoulder.

Landan Mein Sheherzad

Sheher-e-Baghdad ki Sheherzad
Mujh ko Landon ke eik chai-khaane ke andar mili
Uss ka huliya hii badla hua thha
Maine mazhab ki yaksaniyat ka sahara liya
Riwayat ko thhama
Muhabbat se poochha:
'Tumhein apna fun yaad hai?
Dastaanein sunaane ka fun
Vo fun jis se murda-dilon ki kali khil gayi thhi
Vo fun jis se har shab kisi eik ko nayi zindagi mil gayi thhi'

Zara deir ko chup hui Sheherzad
Phir yun goya hui:
'Poori duniya ki maanind tumko khabar hii nahiin
Sheher-e-Baghdad mein ab samaat muattal hui
Log kya lafz bhi mar gaye
Aur mera fun
Samaat ka, lafzon ka muhtaaj hai
Maine ajdaad ki pairwi kii
Raah-e-hijrat pe chalti hui main yahaan aa gayi
Sheher-e-Landan bada meherbaan shehr hai
Yahaan roz-o-shab taaza waarid khalife
Mausamon ke taghayyur ke humrah
Parindon ki maanind aate hain
Mujhko bulaate hain
Mere har moo-e-tan se dastanon ko sunte hain
Aur laut jaate hain.'

Sheherzad in London

I met the Sheherzad of Baghdad
In a teahouse in London
She had changed beyond recognition.
Relying upon the commonality of religion
Holding on to tradition,
I asked her with affection:
'Do you remember your art?
The art of telling stories,
The art that could bring life to lifeless hearts,
The art that revived someone every evening!'

Sheherzad was quiet for a while
Then she said:
'Like the rest of the world, you too don't know.
Meetings have been suspended in the city of Baghdad.
Like people, words too are dead,
And my art is dependent upon meetings, upon words.
Following my ancestors,
Walking the path of *hijrat,* I came here.
The city of London is a benevolent city.
Morning and evening, newly-descended caliphs come here,
Travelling with the change in the seasons.
Like birds
They call me,
They listen to new stories that emerge
From every pore and fibre of my being
And then they go back.'

Zehra Ne Bahut Din Se Kuchh Bhi Nahin Likkha Hai

Zehra ne bahut din se kuchh bhi nahin likkha hai
Halaanki dar-in-asna kya kuchh nahin dekha hai
Par likkhe to kya likkhe? Aur soche to kya soche?
Kuchh fikr bhi mubham hai kuchh haath larazta hai

Zehra ne bahut din se kuchh bhi nahin likkha hai!
Diwaani nahin itni jo munh mein ho bak jaae
Chup Shah ka roza bhi yunhi nahin rakkha hai
Boodhi bhi nahin itni iss tarah vo thak jaae
Ab jaan ke uss ne ye andaaz banaaya hai
Har cheez bhulave ke sandooq mein rakh di hai
Aasaani se jeene ka achchha ye tareeqa hai

Zehra ne bahut din se kuchh bhi nahin likkha hai!
Ghar baar, samajhti thii, qila hai hifaazat ka
Dekha ki grihasti bhi mitti ka khilauna hai
Mitti ho ki patthar ho hira ho ki moti ho
Ghar-baar ke malik ka ghar-baar pe qabza hai
Ehsas-e-hukumat ke izhaar ka kya kahna!
Inaam hai mazhab ka jo haath mein koda hai

Zehra ne bahut din se kuchh bhi nahin likkha hai!
Deewar pe tanga thha farmaan rifaaqat ka
Kya waqt ke dariya ne deewar ko dhaaya hai
Farman-e-rifaaqat ki taqdees bas itni hai
Ik jumbish-e-lab par hai, rishta jo azal ka hai

Zehra Has Not Written Anything at All for Many Days

Zehra has not written anything at all for many days,
Although there's much that she has seen in this time.
If she were to write, what can she write? And what can she think?
Her thoughts are a bit ambiguous, her hands shake somewhat.

Zehra has not written anything at all for many days.
She's not so foolish that she will spit out whatever is on her tongue.
It isn't lightly that she has taken this fast of silence,
Nor is she so old that she will tire easily.
This manner, it's a deliberate choice.
She has put away everything in the Trunk of Forgetfulness,
It is a good way to live life, easily, simply.

Zehra has not written anything at all for many days.
Her home and hearth, she always thought, were her Fortress of Safety,
But even domesticity, she's seen, is merely a toy made of clay.
Be it clay or stone, diamond or pearl,
It is the owner of the house who has control over the household.
And what can one say of the expression of this sense of power!
The whip in that hand is the reward of religion.

Zehra has not written anything at all for many days.
The edict of friendship was hung on the wall
But look how the river of Time has demolished the wall.
The sanctity of that edict is merely this:
It sits on the quivering lip, this bond that is as old as Time.

Zehra ne bahut din se kuchh bhi nahin likkha hai!
Do beton ko kya paala nadaan ye samajhti thhi
Iss daulat-e-duniya ki malik wahi tanha hai
Par waqt ne aaina kuchh aisa dikhaaya hai
Tasweer ka ye pahlu ab saamne aaya hai
Badhte hue bachchon par khulti hui duniya hai
Khulti hui duniya ka har baab tamasha hai
Maa baap ki surat to dekha hua naqsha hai
Dekhe hue naqshe ka har rang puraana hai

Zehra ne bahut din se kuchh bhi nahin likkha hai!
Socha thha bahan bhai dariya hain mohabbat ke
Dekha ki kabhi dariya rasta bhi badalta hai
Bhai bhi giraftar-e-majboori-e-ḳhidmat hain
Bahnon pe bhi taari hai qismat ka jo likkha hai
Ik maa hai jo perhon se baatein kiye jaati hai
Kahne ko hain dus bachche aur phir bhi vo tanha hai

Zehra ne bahut din se kuchh bhi nahin likkha hai

Zehra has not written anything at all for many days.
In raising two sons the innocent woman thought
She alone is the owner of all the wealth of the world,
But Time has shown her such a mirror
And revealed such facets in that image!
The growing children have the world opening up for them,
Every chapter of this unfurling world presents new spectacles;
The faces of mothers and fathers are familiar maps;
The colours of old maps, worn with use, are faded.

Zehra has not written anything at all for many days.
Her brothers and sisters, she thought, were rivers of love
But rivers change their course sometimes.
The brothers are helpless captives of service,
The sisters are overwhelmed by what is written in their fate.
And then there is the mother who talks to trees;
She who has ten children and yet is so lonely.

Zehra has not written anything at all for many days.

Vo Kitaab

Miri zindagi ki likhi hui
Mire taq-e-dil pe saji hui
Vo kitab ab bhi hai muntazir
Jise main kabhi nahin padh saki

Vo tamaam baab sabhi varaq
Hain abhi talak bhi judey hue
Mira ahd-e-deed bhi aaj tak
Unhein vo judaai na de saka
Jo har ik kitab ki ruuh hai

Mujhe ḳhauf hai ki kitaab mein
Mire roz-o-shab ki aziyyatein
Vo nadaamatein vo malaamatein
Kisi hashiye pe raqam naa hon
Main fareb-ḳhurda-e-bartari
Main aseer-e-halqa-e-buz-dili
Vo kitaab kaise padhungi main?

That Book

Written by my life,
Placed in the niche of my heart,
That book is still waiting,
The book I've never read.

All those chapters, all those pages
Are still stuck together, still unopened.
My reading eye
Has not yet given them the separation
That is the spirit of any book.

I fear in that book
All the troubles of my nights and days
All the regrets and reproaches
Might be marked in the margins somewhere.
I, who am deceived by my sense of superiority
I, who am a captive in my circle of cowardice—
How will I ever read that book?

Eik Ladki

Kaisa saḳht toofan thha
Kitni tez barish thhi
Aur main aise mausam mein
Jaane kyuun bhatakti thhi
Vo sadak ke uss janib
Raushni ke khambe se
Sar lagae istada
Aane waale gaahak ke
Intizar mein gum thhi
Khal-o-ḳhaad ki araaish
Bah rahi thhi baarish mein
Tiir nok-e-mizhgaan ke
Mil gae thhe mitti mein
Gesuon ki ḳhush-rangi
Urh rahi thhi jhonkon mein
Main ne dil mein ye socha
Aab-o-baad ka rela
Uss ko raakh kar dega
Ye saja bana chehra
Kya daravna hoga
Phir bhi uss ko le jaana
Aane waale gaahak ka
Apna hausla hoga

A Girl

What a terrible storm it was!
How hard the rain came down!
And I don't know why
I wandered about in this weather.

There she stood, across the road from me,
Leaning her head against the lamp-post,
Lost in thought
Waiting for the next client.
The paint on her face
Was washed away in the rain,
The pointed arches of her eyebrows, too
All gone by now.
Her brightly coloured hair
Flew about ragged in the wind.
I thought to myself:
Surely, this surge of wind and rain
Will reduce her to mud and ash.
The painted, made-up face undone—
How frightful it will look.
Still, if her next client
Were to take her away,
He must be a man of courage.

Barishon ne jab uss ka
Rang-o-roop dho daala
Main ne darte darte phir
Uss ko ġhaur se dekha
Seedha-saada chehra thha
Bhola-bhala naqsha tha
Rang-e-kamsini jis par
Kaise dhul ke aaya thha
Zard phool sa patta
Gesuon mein uljha thha
Shabnami sa ik qatra
Aankh par larazta thha
Raakh ki jagah uss ka
Ik diya sa jalta thha

Mujh ko yuun laga aise
Jaise meri beti ho
Meri naaz ki paali
Meri kokh-jai ho

Daal se bandha jhoola
Taaq mein saji gudiyan
Ghar mein chhorh aai ho
Tez tez chalne par
Main ne uss ko toka ho
Haath thaam lene par
Mera uss ka jhagda ho
Kho gai ho mele mein
Bah gai ho rele mein
Aur phir andhere mein
Apne ghar ka darwaza
Khud na dekh paai ho!

But when the rain had
Quite washed her clean,
Fearfully, I looked closely at her face.
It was an ordinary, artless face,
Naive in features,
Coloured with tender innocence.
A lone yellow leaf, like a flower,
Was tangled in her hair.
Like dew, a drop of rain
Quivered on her eye,
And instead of looking ashen
Her face glowed like a lamp.

And I felt as though
She were my daughter,
Born from my womb,
Whom I had raised with love.
Who had left behind at home
A swing hanging from a branch
And dolls sitting in an alcove;
Whom I had scolded
For walking too fast;
Who had pulled her hand out of mine then;
Who had got lost in a fair, then;
Who had been swept up in the crowd
And had missed the door
To her home in the darkness.

Dafatan ye dil chaaha
Uss ko gode mein bhar luun
Le ke bhaag jaun main
Haath jorh luun uss ke
Choom luun ye peshani
Aur usse manaaun main
Phir se apne aanchal ka
Ghonsla banaaun main
Aur usse chhupaun main

And suddenly, my heart called out:
To gather her in my lap,
To run away somewhere with her,
To fold my hands in entreaty before her,
To kiss her brow,
To coddle and assuage her;
To make a nest, again,
With the folds of my garment,
To hide her there,
To keep her safe.

Eik Sachchi Amma ki Kahani

Mire bachche ye kahte hain
'Tum aati ho to ghar mein raunaqein ḳhushbuein aati hain
Ye jannat jo mili hai sab unhin qadmon ki barkat hai
Hamare vaaste rakhna tumhaara ik saadat hai'

Badi mushkil se main daaman chhurha kar laut aai huun
Vo aansu aur vo ġhamgeen chehre yaad aate hain
Abhi mat jaao ruk jaao ye jumle sataate hain

Main ye saari kahani aane valon ko sunaati huun
Mire lahje se lipta jhuut sab pahchaan jaate hain
Bahut tahzeeb waale log hain sab maan jaate hain

The Tale of a Truthful Mother

My children say:
'When you come, brightness and fragrance come to our house.
This heaven that we have found is because of these feet.
To have you stay with us is our great good fortune.'

With much difficulty have I wrenched myself free and returned.
I remember those tears and those sorrowful faces:
'Don't go just yet, stay.' How those pleas torment me!

I tell this entire tale to all those who come to meet me.
Everyone recognises the falsehood entwined in my speech.
But they are decent people; they agree with everything I say.

Shaam ka Pahla Taara—I

Jab jhonka tez havaon ka
Kuchh soch ke dheeme guzra thha
Jab tapte suraj ka chehra
Oodi chaadar mein lipta thha
Jab sookhi mitti ka seena
Sanson ki nami se jaaga thha
Hum log uss shaam ikatthe thhe
Jis ne hamein hans kar dekha thha
Vo pahla dost hamara thha
Vo shaam ka pahla taara thha
Jo shaayad hum donon ke liye
Kuchh waqt se pahle nikla thha
Jab jhilmil karta vo kamra
Cigarette ke dhuein se dhundla thha
Jab nasha-e-mai ki talḳhi se
Har shaḳhs ka lahja meetha thha
Har fikr ki apni manzil thhi
Har soch ka apna rasta thha

Hum log uss raat ikatthe thhe
Uss raat bhi kya hangama thha
Main mahv-e-mudarat-e-alam
Aur tum ko zauq-e-tamasha thha
Mauzu-e-suḳhan jis par hum ne
Raae dii thhi aur socha thha
Duniya ki badalti halat thhi
Kuchh aab-o-hawa ka qissa thha
Jab sab logon ki aankhon mein
Kamre ka dhuan bhar aaya thha
Tab main ne khidki kholi thhi
Tum ne parda sarkaya thha
Jis ne hamein dukh se dekha thha
Vo pahla dost hamara thha
Vo shaam ka pahla taara thha

The First Star of the Evening—I

When a gust of strong wind
Had paused briefly in thought as it passed,
When the face of the blistering sun
Had wrapped itself in a purple cloak,
When the breast of the dry earth
Had come awake with the dampness of breaths—
We were together that evening.
He who had looked at us, laughing,
He was our first friend;
He was the first star of the evening.
He had come out a little earlier than usual, perhaps
Just for the two of us.
When that shimmering room
Was hazy with the smoke of cigarettes,
When the bitterness of intoxicating wines
Had sweetened every tongue in the gathering,
When every concern had its destination
And every thought its own pathway—
We were together that night.

What a furore there was that night.
I was engrossed in the worldly courtesies of the hostess,
And you in the pleasure of beholding the spectacle.
The topic of conversation, on which
We'd expended our thoughts and expressed our opinions,
Was the changing affairs of the world,
The ways and the weather of the world,
Till the smoke in the room got into everyone's eyes
And I'd opened the window
And you had nudged aside the curtain,
And he who had looked upon us with sadness then,
He was our first friend;
He was the first star of the evening.

Jo shayad hum donon ke liye
Uss raat sahar tak jaaga thha

Vo shaam ka pahla taara thha

He had stayed awake all night till daybreak, perhaps
Just for the two of us.

He was the first star of the evening.

'Alif' or 'Bey' Ke Naam

Jaanan! Kya ye ho sakta hai
Aaj ki shaam kahin nahin jaayein
Shor machaaney waley feetey
Awaazon se bharey tawe
Sab thorhi der ko chup ho jaayein
Janaan! Kya ye ho sakta hai?

Iss pyazi mashroob ke paimaney bhi na chhalkein
Jin ke bal pe hamaari khush-akhlaqui
Aam hui hai
Aur naa mozuaat ke laave munh se ublein
Aisey log ke jinke chehrey bahut barhe or dil chhote hain
Aaj hamein surat na dikhayein
Thorhi der ko tanhai ki halki khunki basi rahey
Log gharon mein or botal almaari mein saji rahe

Hum donon iss kamrey mein hon
Jiski deewaron pe hamaarey sukh ke bandhan
Tasweeron ki shakl mein aawezaan rahte hain
Jismey rakhkhey kaath ke ghorey
Kot ke haathi
Sab humko takte rahte hain
Jisme baithee kaanch ki chirhyan
Humko dekh ke dar sii gai hain
Jismey rakhkhi kai kitaabein
Humse rooth ke mar sii gai hain
Hum donon tanha hon
Thorhi der ko gum sum se betheyein

Phir rafta rafta baat-cheet ke
Chhotey chhotey phool khilein
Qurbat ki garmi se pashemaani ke aansu
Diye ki tarah se jal uthey

Dedicated to 'A' and 'B'

My darling, can it be
That we don't go anywhere this evening,
That the clamorous measuring tapes
And griddles laden with voices
Should all fall silent for some time?
My darling, can it be so

That the goblets of this pink wine—the reason why
Our good behaviour is so well known—do not overflow,
Nor lavas of conversation erupt from our mouth?
That people whose faces are too big and hearts small
Should not appear before us today,
That the cool breath of solitude should pervade for a little while,
That people should stay in their homes and
    the wine-bottle in the cupboard?

The two of us should be in the room
On whose walls the bonds of our happiness
Hang like paintings,
The room where wooden horses and elephants*
Keep gazing at us,
Where the glass birds sit frozen
As if afraid at the sight of us,
Where the books have died a little,
Neglected and angry with us,
Where the two of us can be alone
And sit awhile in a silence.

And gradually, gradually
The flowers of small talk will blossom,
The warmth of closeness cause tears of repentance
To light up like lamps.

---

*.The reference is to the Knight and Bishop in the game of chess

Janaan kya ye ho sakta hai?
Ab bhi mera dil kahta hai
Shayad aisa ho sakta hai

My darling, can it be so?
My heart still says
It can be so.

Mata-e-Alfaaz

Ye jo tum mujh se gurezan ho miri baat suno

Hum isi chhoti si duniya ke kisi raaste par
Ittifaqan kabhi bhoole se kahin mil jaaen
Kya hii achchha ho ki hum doosre logon ki tarah
Kuchh takalluf se sahi thahar ke kuchh baat karein

Aur iss arsa-e-aḳhlaq-o-murawwat mein kabhi
Ek pal ke liye vo saat-e-naazuk aa jaae
Naḳhun-e-lafz kisi yaad ke zaḳhmon ko chhue
Ik jhijakta hua jumla koi dukh de jaae
Kaun jaanega ki hum donon pe kya beeti hai
Iss ḳhamoshi ke andheron se nikal aaen chalo
Kisi sulge hue lahje se charaġhaan kar lein
Chun lein phulon ki tarah hum bhi mata-e-alfaaz
Apne ujde hue daaman ko gulistan kar lein
Chun lein phoolon ki tarah hum bhi mata-e-alfaaz
Daulat-e-dard badi cheez hai iqraar karo
Nemat-e-ġham badi nemat hai ye izhaar karo
Lafz paimaan bhi iqraar bhi izhaar bhi hain
Taaqat-e-sabr agar ho to ye ġham-ḳhvar bhi hain
Haath ḳhaali hon to ye jins-e-giraan-bar bhi hain
Paas koi bhi na ho phir to ye dildaar bhi hain

Ye jo tum mujh se gurezan ho miri baat suno

The Commodity of Words

You, who are avoiding me, listen to me.

On some path in this small world
If we were perchance to meet somewhere, someday,
Wouldn't it be nice if we were to stop awhile
And like people do, talk a little, even if with some formality?
And during this time of politeness and civility,
If even for an instant that delicate moment comes
When the nail of words grazes the wound of memories,
A faltering sentence causes some sorrow,
Who will know what has befallen us?
Come, let us emerge from the darkness of silence
Let us light the lamp with some lit intonations
Let us pick, like flowers, the commodity of words
Let us turn our barren world into a flower garden
Let us confess that the wealth of pain is a great fortune
Let us declare that the boon of sorrow is a great blessing.
Words can be a promise, a confession, a revelation,
And if you have the power of patience, they can be a comfort,
And if your hands are empty, they can be the dearest of goods,
And if no one is beside you, they can be your beloved too.

You, who are avoiding me, listen to me.

Daaku

Kal raat mira beta mire ghar
Chehre pe moondhe ḳhaki kapda
Bandooq uthae aa pahuncha
Nau-umri ki surḳhi se rachi uss ki ankhein
Main jaan gai
Aur bachpan ke sandal se mandha uss ka chehra
Pahchan gai
Vo aaya thha ḳhud apne ghar
Ghar ki cheezein le jaane ko
Ankahi kahi manwaane ko

Baaton mein doodh ki ḳhushbu thhi
Jo kuchh bhi saint ke rakkha thha
Main saari cheezein le aai
Ik laal-e-badaḳhshan ki chidiya
Sone ka haath chhota sa
Chandi ki ik nannhi taḳhti
Resham ki phool bhari topi
Atlas ka naam likha juzdaan
Juzdaan mein lipta ik Quran
Par vo kaisa diwaana thha
Kuchh chhorh gaya kuchh torh gaya
Aur le bhi gaya hai vo to kya
Lohe ki bad-surat gaarhi
Petrol ki bu bhi aaegi
Jis ke pahiye bhi rubber ke hain
Jo baat nahin kar paegi
Bachcha phir aaḳhir bachcha hai

Dacoit

One night my son came to my house,
A khaki cloth wound around his face
A gun in his hand,
But I saw
The red glow of adolescence in his eyes
And recognised the dusky gleam of childhood on his face.
He had come to his own home,
To take away our household goods,
To make me agree to his unsaid words.

His words smelled of milk.
I brought whatever I had,
Collected carefully over the years:
A bird made of blood-red ruby
A tiny golden hand
A small silver slate
A silken cap adorned with flowers
A brocade cover—with his name—for the Holy Book
And wrapped in it, a Quran.
But he was so foolish.
Some things he took, others he broke,
And among the things he took
Was an ugly car made of metal
That will no doubt reek of petrol.
Its wheels are made of rubber,
They will not be able to talk.
The child is, after all, a child.

Eik Tilismi Khel

Kaise kaise naam likhe thhe
Waqt ne maah-o-saal ke ruḳh par
Toofanon ne paala maara
Saare ho gae tittar-bittar
Saiqal kar ke rakhna chaha
Hum ne kuchh naamon ko bacha kar
Umr ki maujein bahaa le gaiin
Saare laal aur saare jawahir

Tarz-e-ḳhiram ke phool khile thhe
Aati jaati rahguzar par
Aaj hai sirf ġhubaar ka parda
Kaisi manzil kaisa manzar
Dhajji dhajji bikhar rahi hai
Tani hui ehsas ki chaadar
Kuchh harfon ki maddham si lau
Kaanp rahi hai laraz laraz kar
Khushbu apni kho baitha hai
Sab sheron ka mushk aur ambar
Surat apni badal chuke hain

Ahd aqide masjid mimbar
Kaise ḳhaali haath khade hain
Shah vazeer ameer gadagar
Ujdi ḳhwaab-o-ḳhayal ki duniya
Apne gharon mein sab hain be-ghar
Kyun-kar jodein apne tukde
Haar gae hain saare rafugar
Khuni baadal gahre gahre
Chhate nahin hain baras baras kar

A Magical Game

So many wondrous names were written
By Time on the face of the months and years
But the storms struck
And they scattered in the winds.
We tried to save some names
And keep them burnished.
But the waves of age carried them away,
All the rubies and all the jewels.

Flowers of every kind once bloomed
Along the paths that came up to us
And those that swept away.
Now there's only the veil of dust
Before us, neither destination nor spectacle.
The sheet of feeling stretched tight
Disintegrates shred by shred,
The lambent flame of words, a few words,
Sputters, quivers and trembles.
And the musk and amber of all the verses
Are now bereft of fragrance.

Time, tenets, mosque and pulpit
Have changed their forms and faces,
And look how empty handed they stand—
All the rulers, nobles and mendicants.
Our world of dreams and thoughts laid waste,
We are all homeless in our homes,
Why bother mending the torn pieces,
All the darners have accepted defeat.

Dark, massed, blood-soaked clouds
Haven't cleared, though it has poured and poured

Aur zameenein aankhein moonde
Mast hui hain lahu pee pee kar

Ek tilismi khel racha hai
Jaane kaun hai ye jadugar

And the lands, eyes closed, are swooning,
Intoxicated with blood.

A magical game has played out.
Who is the magician? Who knows.

Ye Khaal-o-Khad Mere Apne

Har ek jism mira hai, har ek jaan miri
Ye k̤haal-o-k̤had mire apne, ye aan-baan meri
Sitam to ye hai ki mazloom main huun zaalim main
Har ek zak̤hm mujhi se hisaab maangega
Har ek daag̈h miri aasteen se jhaankega

Hazaar-ha miri peshaniyon ke chaand bujhe
Hazaar-ha mire lab hum-kanaar-e-zahr hue
Hazaar-ha mire jismon ki daaliyan tootiin
Hazaar-ha miri aankhon ki mishalein doobiin

Jahaan pe aag lagi hai, wahan khilaune thhe
Jahaan pe k̤haak udi hai, wahan pe jhoole thhe
Jahaan pe sard hain seene wahan pe chaukhat thhi
Jahaan pe band hain aankhein wahan dareeche thhe
Main iss dhuen mein kahaan apni laash ko dhoondun
Main iss hujoom mein kaise shumaar-e-zak̤hm karun

Sitam to ye hai ki mazloom main huun, zaalim main
Har ek zak̤hm mujhi se hisaab maangega
Har ek daag̈h miri aasteen se jhaankega

This Form and These Features Are My Own

Each body is mine, every life is mine,
This form and these features are my own, this beauty
    and grace are mine.
Such is the injustice that I am the oppressed and the oppressor too,
Every wound will ask only me for recompense
Every stain will show itself from behind my sleeve.

Countless times the moon of my forehead waned
Countless times my lips came close to touching poison.
Countless times the boughs of my body broke
Countless times the torches of my eyes were snuffed out.

Where the fire rages, once there were toys.
Where dust swirls, once there were swings.
These hearts that are cold, once they were thresholds,
These eyes that are shut, once they were windows.
Where shall I search for my corpse in this smoke?
How shall I count my wounds in this crowd?

Such is the injustice that I am the oppressed and the oppressor too,
Every wound will ask only me for recompense
Every stain will show itself from behind my sleeve

Naya Ghar

Kahin duur basti ki aġhosh mein
Vo humakta hua ik naya ghar
Apne atraaf se be-ḳhabar
Nanhe bachche ke maanind hansta hua
Ik naye-pan ki ḳhushbu mein basta hua
Hamesha mujhe aur tum ko bulaata rahega
Apni mutthi ke ghunghru bajaata rahega

Vo naya ghar jo mera tumhara nahin thha
Kisi taur se bhi hamara nahin thha
Koocha koocha bhatakte hue jis ke dar par
Thakey-harey hum tum shikasta-dil o ḳhak-basar
Tan pe baar-e-nadamat uthaaye hue ruk gaye thhe
Uss ke diwaar-o-dar farsh-o-aangan
Hamein dekh kar kis tarah jhuk gae thhe
Uss ke phaile hue baazuon ne
Hamein iss tarah se samoya
Aur aisi jagah dii
Ki chehron ki mitti rifaaqat ki afshan bani
Aur nadaamat ki zardi na jaane kahan mit gayi
Mujh ko aisa laga jaise anmol moti
Tah-e-aab se mauj-dar-mauj ladta hua
Khud kinaare tak aaye
Apna ḳhakistari ḳhol suraj ki tahvil mein de ke
Saari thakan bhuul jaaye
Phir shua-e-mohabbat se saara jahan jagmagaye
Mere dil ne dua di ḳhudavand-e-bartar:
Issi raushni mein nahaata rahe ye naya ghar
Apni mutthi ke ghunghru bajaata rahe ye naya ghar
Humari tarah doosre dil-zadon ko bulaata rahe ye naya ghar

New House

Somewhere far away, in the lap of some habitation
That new house, toddling
Heedless of its surroundings
Laughing like a little child,
Swathed in the fragrance of novelty,
Will always call out to you and to me
Rattling the tinkling bells in its fists.

That new house that was neither yours nor mine,
In no way was it ours.
Having wandered high and low
We had arrived at its door
Tired, broken hearted, distressed and destitute
Carrying the weight of repentance on our bodies
We had paused.
How its walls, floors and courtyard
Had bowed upon seeing us;
Its widespread arms had embraced us
And given us so much space
That the dirt on our faces turned into the tinsel of friendship
And the pallor of reproach vanished who knows where.
And I had felt as though a priceless pearl had
Reached the shore all on its own
Fighting wave after wave from the depths of the waters,
And having given its ash-coloured shell to the custody of the sun,
Forgetting all its fatigue,
Had dazzled the world with rays of love.
And my heart prayed: O Lord of Lords
May this new house always bathe in this light!
May this new house keep rattling the tinkling bells in its fists!
May this new house keep calling out to other bruised
hearts like ours!

Ab to Kuchh Aisa Lagta Hai

Ab to kuchh aisa lagta hai
Saara jag mujh se chhota hai
Aaankhein bhi miri bojhal bojhal
Shaanon par bhi kuchh rakkha hai
Kaatib-e-waqt ne jaate jaate
Chehre par kuchh likh sa diya hai
Aaine mein chehra khole
Dekh rahi huun kya likhkha hai

Likhkha hai tire roop ka haala
Aur kisi ke gird saja hai
Likhkha hai zulfon ka do-shala
Aur kisi ne odh liya hai
Likhkha hai aankhon ka pyala
Kahin kahin se tuut raha hai

Padh kar mushaf-e-rukh ki ibaarat
Dil ko itminaan hua hai
Ruuh talak sarshaar hai meri
Aaiina hairaan hua hai
Uss ko shaayad ilm nahin hai
Mera daaman ab bhi bhara hai
Jo rakhna thha rakkhe hue huun
Jo dena thha baant diya hai

Now It Seems as Though

Now it seems as though
The entire world is smaller than me.
My eyes are heavy, there is a weight
On my shoulders too.
As it passed by, Time, the Writer,
Has written something on my face;
With my face exposed to the mirror
I'm trying to read what He has written.

He has written: The nimbus of your beauty
Adorns someone else.
He has written: The shawl of your hair
Is worn by someone else.
He has written: The bowls of your eyes
Are chipped in places.

Reading the inscription on the pages of my face
My heart is content,
My soul brims over with joy.
But the mirror is perplexed.
Perhaps it doesn't know
My lap is still full;
I've kept what I had to keep
I've given away what I had to give away.

Shaam ka Pehla Taara—II

Meri us shaam ke taare se mulaqaat bahut gahri thhi
Vo mira hum-dam-e-derina thha
Main bahut chhoti thhi jab maa ne bataya thha mujhe
'Dekho dekho vo udhar vo miri ungli ke qareeb
Ek taara bhi tumhein dekhta hai'

Unn dinon jab main havaon ki tarah udti thhi
Aur daali ki tarah jhuum ke lahraati thhi
Raat aur din ke lipatne ki gharhi aate hii
Sirf uss taare ki ḳhatir main thahar jaati thhi
Vo mujhe dekhta thha
Main bhi usse dekhti thi
Vo mujhe dhoondhta thha
Main bhi usse dhoondhti thhi
Aur uss eid-e-mulaqaat ke baad
Roz hum donon bichhad jaate thhe

Apni manzil ki taraf vo bhi chala jaata thha
Apne raston ki taraf main bhi palat aati thhi

Meri uss shaam ke taare se mulaqat bahut gahri thhi
Main ne taare ki rifaaqat mein shagun kitne liye
Aaj dekha nahin taara main ne
Aaj ki shaam jo roz aata hai shaayad nahin aae
Rasta bhool na jaae
Aaj to jald nikal aaya hai taara mera
Aaj ki raat mulaqaat milegi mujh ko
An-kahe lafzon ki sauġhaat milegi mujh ko
Main ne taare ki rifaaqat mein shagun kitne liye

The First Star of the Evening—II

My meeting with that evening star was an old and intimate one,
He was my companion and friend.
I was very young when my mother told me:
'Look! Look, there, there near my finger
A star too is looking at you.'

Those days when I wafted like the breeze
And swayed like a bough,
As the moment approached when night and day would embrace
I would stop still.
He would look at me
And I too would look at him.
He would search for me,
I too would search for him.
And after the happiness of meeting
Every day, the two of us would part.

He would go away towards his destination
And I too would return to my paths.

My meeting with that evening star was an old and intimate one,
I read so many omens in my friendship with that star:
Today, I haven't seen the star;
He who comes every day might not come today;
What if he loses his way?
Today, my star has appeared sooner than usual;
Tonight, I too shall find my union,
I shall receive the rare gift of unsaid words…
I read so many omens in my friendship with that star.

Ab main tanha huun
Baras beet gae hain kitne
Koi taara nahin dekha main ne
Duur ki cheez zara dhundli nazar aati hai
Apne aanchal mein usse baandh liya
Bhala iss umr mein ye saath kisey milta hai

Meri uss shaam ke taare se mulaqaat bahut gahri thhi
Mira humdam-e-derina thha...
Meri ḳhwavabeeda samaat ko jagaane ke liye
Sirf awaaz-e-azaan aati hai
Ab shagun kaahe se luun
Kis ke aane ki umidein bandhun
Kis ke jaane se pareshan rahun

Kal magar phone ki ghanti ne mujhe
Apne mahaul se bedaar kiya
Zindagi se mujhe do-char kiya
Ek amrit bhara lahja mire kaanon mein ghula
'Amma kal shaam dikhaya hum ne
Apne bachchon ko chamakta tara'

'Kaun sa taara dikhaya tum ne?'

'Aap ka shaam ka pahla tara'

Phone jab ḳhatm hua
Waqt donon hi gale milte thhe
Main ne khidki se hataaya parda
Aasman hadd-e-nazar tak waraq-e-sada thha

I am alone now.
So many years have passed,
I haven't seen any star.
Far-off things appear somewhat hazy.
And tied him in the folds of my hem
After all, who gets such companionship at this age?

My meeting with that evening star was an old and intimate one...
My companion, my friend.
The only sound that comes to waken my somnolent senses
Is the call to prayer.
Where should I look for omens?
The hope of whose coming should I shore up?
At whose going away should I fret?

But the sound of the telephone yesterday
Woke me up
And brought me face to face with life.
A sweet-as-nectar voice filled my ears:
'Amma, last evening I showed
The bright star to my children.'

'Which star did you show?'
'Your first star of the evening.'

By the time the phone call ended
Night and day were meeting in an embrace.
I pushed aside the curtain from the window,
The sky was like a blank page as far as the eye could see.

Na shafaq thhi na ufuq par hi koi taara thha
Yak-ba-yak ek kiran chehre par lahraane lagi
Duur ki cheez zara dhundli nazar aati hai
Mera taara meri palkon par utar aaya thha
Main ne ungli ke sahare se usse thaam liya

There were no twilight colours nor was there a star
on the distant horizon.
But suddenly a ray of light reached my face.
Distant things appear somewhat hazy;
My star had descended upon my lashes.
I held him on the tip of my finger

Aaj Ki Baat

Aaj ki baat nai baat nahin hai aisi
Jab kabhi dil se koi guzra hai yaad aayi hai
Sirf dil hii ne nahin gode mein ḳhamoshi ki
Pyaar ki baat to har lamhe ne dohrai hai

Chupke chupke hii chatakhne do ishaaron ke gulaab
Dheeme dheeme hii sulagne do taqaazon ke alaav
Rafta rafta hii chhalakne do adaaon ki sharaab
Dheere dheere hii nigaahon ke ḳhazaane bikhraao

Baat achchhi ho to sab yaad kiya karte hain
Kaam suljha ho to rah rah ke ḳhayaal aata hai
Dard meetha ho to ruk ruk ke kasak hoti hai
Yaad gahri ho to tham tham ke qaraar aata hai

Dil guzargah hai ahista-ḳhirami ke liye
Tez-gami ko jo apnaaoge to kho jaoge
Ik zara der hii palkon ko jhapak lene do
Iss qadar ġhaur se dekhoge to so jaoge

About Today

It isn't just about today,
Whenever someone has gone past my heart,
    I have remembered.
Why just the heart, even my lap has fallen silent
    in remembrance.
Every moment has remembered those things
    to do with love.

Let the roses of signs and gestures bloom silently
Let the bonfire of demands smoulder unhurriedly
Let the wine of affectations brim over drop by drop
Let the treasures of your eyes scatter gradually.

If a thing is good everyone remembers it
If a deed is sober it stays in the mind
If a pain is sweet, it stabs again and again
If a memory is deep, it brings solace, slowly.

The heart is a thoroughfare for the slow moving;
If you pick a fast pace, you will lose your way.
Blink, let your eyes shut at least for an instant;
If you watch so closely you will fall asleep.

Eik Puraani Kahani

Kisi shahr mein ik kafan-chor aaya
Jo raaton ko qabron mein suraaḳh kar ke
Tan-e-kushtagan se kafan kheench leta
Aḳhir-e-kaar pakda gaya
Aur uss ko munasib saza ho gayi

Kuchh hii din baad ik doosra chor varid hua
Jo kafan bhi churata
Qabr ko bhi khuli chhorh deta
Doosra chor bhi rukn-e-insaaf ke paas laaya gaya
Aur mehmaan-e-zindaan hua

Phir yakayak kisi teesre chor ka ġhul macha
Jo kafan bhi churata
Qabr ko bhi khula chhorh deta
Aur murda badan ko barahana kisi raah par daal deta

Shahr waale jab ussey adalat mein laaye
To qaazi ne uss ki saza ko sunaate huwe
Faisla yuun likha:
'Khudavand pahle kafan-chor ko apni rahmat mein rakhna
ki vo aadmi ḳhuub tha'

An Old Story

A thief who stole shrouds came to a city.
He would make holes in the graves at night
And pull the shrouds from the bodies of the dead
Till finally he was caught
And given an appropriate punishment.

A few days later, a second thief appeared
Who would also steal shrouds
And leave the graves open.
He too was brought before the law
And sent to jail.

Suddenly there was a clamour about a third thief
Who would steal shrouds
Leave the graves open
And throw the naked dead bodies on some road somewhere.

When the people of the city brought him to the court,
Pronouncing his judgement, the judge proclaimed:
'O Dear Lord, keep the first thief safe in Your mercy,
for he was a good man!'

Virsa

Murh kar peechhe dekh rahi huun
Kya kya kuchh virse mein mila thha
Aur kya kuchh main chhorh rahi huun

Mera ghar toofan-zada thha
Mere buzurgon ne dekha thha
Vo ifriit-e-waqt ki jis ne
Unn se sab kuchh chheen liya thha
Phir bhi kya kuchh mujh ko mila thha
Chehron par mehnat ki chamak thhi
Aankhon mein ġhairat ki damak thhi
Haath mein haath dharey thhe kaise
Khali haath bharey thhe kaise
Mil-jul kar rahne ki ravish thhi
Zinda rahne ki ḳhwahish thhi
Ye sab kuchh uss ghar se mila thha
Vo ghar jo ik ḳhali ghar thha

Main ne ek bhare kunbe mein
Apne hanste-baste ghar mein
Khauf ka virsa chhorh diya hai
Rishta-e-jurat torh diya hai

Lahjon mein lafzon ki bachat hai
Qurbat mein kitni vahshat hai
Apni ḳhushiyan apne aangan
Apne khilaune apne daaman

Murh kar peechhe dekh rahi huun
Kya kya kuchh virse mein mila thha
Aur kya kuchh main chhorh rahi huun

Legacy

I'm looking back to see
All that I received as legacy
And all that I'm leaving behind.

My home was wrecked by storms,
My ancestors had seen
The demon of the age
That snatched everything from them.
And yet there was much that I received:
There was the lustre of hard work on their faces
There was the gleam of self-respect in their eyes.
Their hands rested on each other, yet
How full were those hands!
And the habit of living together amicably—
All this I received from that home,
The home that was an empty house.

In my own large family,
In my happy home,
I have bequeathed fear.
I have broken the bonds of courage.

There is an economy of words in what is said
And such dread in nearness,
Everyone with their own joys, their separate spaces,
Their own toys, their own being.

I'm looking back to see
All that I received as legacy
And all that I'm leaving behind.

Aangan

Dar deewar dariche aangan
Dahlizein daalaan aur kamre
Saare roop ye kitne nazuk
Socho to mitti ke khilaune
Mere liye ye kunj-e-ibadat
Mere liye ye koh-e-sadaqat
Mere liye ye manzil-e-waada
Khuld-e-tahaffuz qasr-e-rifaaqat
Jis ke raaj-singhasan baithi
Main rani huun main bechari
Baahar chaahe toofan aayein
Lekin yaan sab chain se soein
Jab jagein tab suraj nikle
So jaaen tab chandni mahke
Mere ghar waale japte hain
Mere naam ki jai-malain
Lakshmi chhaya jaanein mujh ko
Saraswati sa maanein mujh ko
Chaand dekh ke mujh ko dekhein
Hariyali par mujhe chalaayein
Apna taḳht aur taj sambhaale
Shaal doshale kandhon daale
Baal baal moti pirvauun
Pore pore mein heere pahnun
Kaam-kaj ka pallu daale
Din bhar ghar se uljhan suljhan
Raat ko lekin ankhein munde
Pichhli rut ka savaan dekhun

Courtyard

Doors, windows, walls, this courtyard,
Thresholds, verandahs and rooms:
So delicate in all their forms,
Yet mere toys of clay if you think of it.
For me, they are the arbours of worship.
For me, they are the mountain of truth.
For me, they are the promised land.
Like a queen, a poor queen,
I am ensconced upon my throne.
Whatever storms may rage outside
All must sleep in peace inside,
The sun must rise when they rise
And moonlight spread its fragrance when they sleep.
My family chant my name
Telling the beads of their rosaries;
They consider me the spirit of Lakshmi,
They think of me as Saraswati incarnate,
Their eyes seek me after viewing the moon*,
They make me walk on soft verdure.
Holding on to my crown and throne,
My shoulders draped with shawls and stoles,
My hair braided with pearls
And diamonds in every pore,
I'm draped in the muslin of household chores.

All day I am engrossed in domesticity
But at night when I close my eyes
I see the springs of seasons past.

---

*According to a popular South Asian tradition, after viewing the moon, especially the new moon, elders in the family would seek to set eyes on a young and beautiful girl.

Heere laal bikhaarte jaaen
Mahl do mahle hat-te jaaen
Chhota aangan neeche kamre
Duur duur se haath hilaaen
Biite lamhe jugnu jaise
Udte aur chamakte aaen
Mutthi baandh ke unn ko dekhun
Champa phool mahakte jaaen
Jagmag jagmag sone jaisa
Ghar sab ki nazron mein aaya
Bheega aanchal phaila kaajal
Kis ne dekha kis ne chhupaya

Then the diamonds and rubies scatter,
The palaces and mansions fade away,
A small courtyard and low-ceilinged rooms
Wave to me from a distance.
Moments past, like fireflies,
Come flickering brightly,
I catch them in my fists and look at them.
The fragrance of *champa* flowers wafts in.
And glimmering bright as gold
A house hoves into view for all to see.
The damp edge of the veil, the smudged *kajal* of the eyes—
Who saw that? Who hid it?

Khaali Botal

Eik larki se mainey poocha
Khushbu ki yeh khaali botal
Itney sambhaal ke
Kyun rakhi hai
Hans ke boli:

'Zehra apa
Kuch din pahley
Eik barha jinn
Iss botal me qaid raha thha'

'Ab vo kahan hai?'

'Ab vo mahlon ka qaidi hai
Bechare ki qismat dekho
Uskey mahal bhi sheeshey ke hain'

Empty Bottle

I asked a girl:
'Why have you kept
This empty bottle of perfume
So carefully?'

She laughed and said:
'Zehra Aapa
A huge jinn
Was captive in this bottle
Till a few days ago.'

'Where is he now?'

'Now he's a prisoner of palaces.
Look at the poor fellow's fate
His palace too is made of glass!'

Kahani Gul Zamina Ki

Gul Zamina
Suno
Toda-e-ḳhak par
Apni konpal si ungli se
Kya likh rahi ho?
Gul Zamina ne sharbat bhari aankhein oopar uthaain
    aur kahne lagii:
'Kuchh hii din qabl
Ye toda-e-ḳhak hii mera school thha
Main ne Allah ka naam
Ya Hafizo
Uss ki deewar par likh diya thha
Mere kaaġhaz, qalam aur kitabein
Mere kunbe ke humrah sab mit chuke hain

'Main yahan roz aati huun
Apni yaadon ke baste se
Pichhle sabaq dhundhti huun
Safha-e-ḳhak par unn ko likhti huun
Aur laut jaati huun
Meri qismat mein padhna nahin hai
Na ho!
Mera amoḳhta
Mera likhna to jaari rahe'

The Story of Gul Zamina

Gul Zamina!
Listen,
What are you writing
With your bud-like finger
On this heap of dirt?

Gul Zamina raised her hazel eyes
And said:
'Just a few days ago
This heap of dirt was my school.
I had written the name of Allah
Ya Hafiz*
On its wall.
My books, pens and papers
Are all gone,
Like my companions
From my clan.

'I come here every day,
I search for past lessons
In the satchel of my memories,
I write them on the pages of dirt
And go back.
So what if I am not destined to read?
Let it be so!
At least I can continue
To revise what I was taught.'

---

*One of the 99 names of Allah in Arabic meaning 'The Protector'

Eik Gudiya ki Dastaan

Dafli bajaane wala bandar
Ludak gaya, aur duur gira
Lekin dafli bajti rahi...
Chhuk-chhuk karne wali gaadi
Ulat gayi, pahiye ghoome
Phir bhi gaadi chalti rahi
Naachne wala bhalu
Neeche kood gaya aur naacha bhi...
Uski topi hilti, rang badalti rahi
Jeeti jaagti bolne waali gudiya
Aise soyi ke phir boli nahin
Jaagi bhi nahin
Saari duniya aankhein khole takti rahi

A Doll's Tale

The monkey beating the drum
Toppled over and fell far away
But the drum kept beating,
The train chugging along
Turned over, its wheels up,
Yet it kept moving,
The dancing bear
Jumped down and kept dancing,
Its cap kept quivering and changing colours.

A living walking talking doll
Slept so that it never spoke again.
Nor did it wake up
Though the entire world kept looking at it with wide open eyes.

Haath

Baandhni baandhney wali larhki
Pattiyan kaarhney wali larhki
Apney haathon ko jab dekhti hai
Sochti hai ke ye haath merey nahi
Mainey unse dhanak ko chhua
Baandhni mein samoya
Girah baand kar
Apney khawaabon ki rangat chhupa dii
Mainey torha chambeli ka phool
Aanchalon mein piroya
Aur pirotey hi aankhon se shabnam gira dii
Chaand se merey nakhoon
Ulajhtey hue taaron se
Toot-tey aatey jaatey rahe hain
Zakhm suiyyon ke
Pauron mein mehndi lagaatey rahe hain
Iss hatheli pe bikhri lakeerein
Muqaddar ka vo jaal hain
Jin mein ab tak koi phool
Ubhra nahi hai
Koi rang nikhra nahi hai
Rang ras gholtey
Khushbuain baant-tey
Sab se be-rang
Be-ras
Merey haath hain

Hand

The girl who ties *bandhni**
The girl who embroiders leaves
Often looks closely at her hands
And thinks: These are not my hands
I touched the rainbow with these hands
I mixed it in the *bandhni*
By tying a knot
I hid the colours of my dreams
I broke off a *chameli* flower
And threaded it on an *aanchal*
Soon after I've threaded it, the dew drops from my eyes

My moon-like nails
Tangle with the stars
And break often,
The wounds from the needle
Colour my fingertips with henna,
The lines scattered on my palm
Form a web of destiny
Where no flower has bloomed yet,
No colour has burst forth.

Mixing the sap of colours
Scattering fragrances
My hands are
The most colourless of all,
The most devoid of fragrance.

---

*The tie-and-dye craft practiced in several parts of South Asia

Shahr Ke Ek Kushaada Ghar Mein

Shahr ke ek kushaada ghar mein
Apne apne kaam sambhaale
Main aur ek miri tanhai
Hum donon mil kar rahte hain
Baatein karte rote hanste
Har dukh-sukh sahte rahte hain

Aaj ke jab suraj bhi nahin thha
Phulon ke khilne ka ye mausam bhi nahin thha
Aur falak par chand ke chha jaane ka hafta biit chuka thha
Darwaaze ki ghantti ne vo shor machaaya
Jis se puura ghar tharraya

Hum donon hairan hue ki aisa raahi kaun ruka hai
Jo iss ghar ko apna ghar hii samajh raha hai
Khidki se baahar jhaanka to bas ik ḳhwaab sa manzar dekha
Suraj bhi dahleez pe thha
Aur chaand kivaad ki ote se lipta jhaaank raha thha
Phuul khile thhe

Hum ne iss mehman ko sar aankhon pe bithaya
Dil mein jagah dii
Jo apne hum-rah sabhi mausam le aaya
Thhaki hui tanhai ne mujh se
Thhodi deir ko mohlat maangi
Main ne us ko chhutti de dii
Saath mein ye takeed bhi kar dii
Dekho kal tum apne kaam pe jaldi aana
Bhuul na jaana

In a Spacious House in the City

In a spacious house in the city,
Managing our own chores,
My solitude and I
Live together.
We talk, we laugh and cry,
We live through our joys and sorrows.

This day, when there was no sun
Nor was it the season for flowers to bloom
And it wasn't the week for the moon to be splayed
    across the sky, either,
The doorbell created such a din
That it made the entire house tremble.
We were both surprised:
Who could this traveller be?
Who had stopped by?
Who thinks this is his own home?
Peering from the window I saw a dream-like sight:
The sun was at my threshold
The moon was peering in
And flowers had bloomed.

We seated this guest on our eyelashes,
Gave him a place in our heart,
He who had brought along all the seasons.
My tired solitude
Asked me for some respite.
I gave it a holiday
But with the injunction:
Look here, come back early to work tomorrow!
Don't forget

Ye raahi jo saare mausam le aate hain
Inn ke raste saari duniya mein jaate hain
Jis aangan mein chalna seekhein
Uss aangan mein ruk nahin paate
Ruk jaaen to thhak jaate hain

These travellers who bring all the seasons with them
Their paths travel all over the world,
They don't stop to stay
In the courtyard in which they have learnt to walk.
If they stop, they grow tired.

Gul-Chandni

Kal shaam yaad aaya mujhe
Aise ki jaise k̤hwaab thha
Koney mein aangan ke mire
Gul-chandni ka perh thha

Main saari saari dopahar
Saae mein uss ke khelti
Phulon ko chhu kar bhaagti
Shaak̤hon se mil kar jhoolti
Iss ke taney mein beesiyon
Lohe ki keelein thiin jadi
Keelon ko mat chhuna kabhi
Taakiid thhi mujh ko yahi
Ye raaz mujh pe faash thha
Iss perh par aaseb thha
Ik mard-e-kaamil ne magar
Aisa amal uss par kiya
Baahar vo aa sakta nahin
Keelon mein uss ko jarh diya
Haan koi keelon ko agar
Kheenchega uupar ki taraf
Aaseb bhi chhut jaaega
Phulon ko bhi kha jaaega
Patton pe bhi mandlaayega
Phir dekhte hii dekhte
Ye ghar ka ghar jal jaega

Iss sahn-e-jism-o-jan mein bhi
Gul-chandni ka perh hai

Gul-Chandni*

Last evening I recalled
As though in a dream
How it grew in a corner
That tree of gul-chandni.

I would play in its shade
All afternoon long.
I would touch its flowers and run.
I would hold its branches and sway.
Into its trunk had been struck
Scores of iron nails
And I was always told:
Don't touch the nails.
A spirit lived in that tree—
The secret was clear to me—
But a wise man had cast
Such a spell over it
That it could not come out,
Trapped by the nails.
But yes, if someone were
To pull the nails outwards
The spirit would be freed.
It would eat up the flowers
And swarm over the leaves
And in the blink of an eye
The entire house would be burnt down.

In the courtyard of my body and life
There is a plant of gul-chandni.

---

*A white fragrant flower of the Gardenia family, it blooms at night and is similar to Jasmine.

Sab phool mere saath hain
Patte mire hamraaz hain
Iss perh ka saaya mujhe
Ab bhi bahut mahboob hai
Iss ke taney mein aaj tak
Aaseb vo mahsur hai
Ye sochti huun aaj bhi
Keelon ko gar chheda kabhi
Aaseb bhi chhut jaega
Patton se kya lena usey
Phulon se kya matlab usey
Bas ghar mira jal jaega

Kya ghar mira jal jaega?

Its flowers are my companions
Its leaves my confidantes,
The shade of this tree
Is still dearly beloved to me.
That spirit is a captive
In its trunk till today
And I sometimes think:
If I were to pry the nails out,
The spirit will be freed.
It won't trouble the leaves
It won't bother the flowers,
Only my house will be burnt to ashes.

Will my house be burnt to ashes?

Muslim-Muslim Fasaadaat

Subh-dam jo dekha thha
Kya hara-bhara ghar thha
Dant-ti hui biwi
Bhaagte hue bachche
Rassiyon ki baanhon mein
Jhoolte hue kapde
Bolte hue bartan
Jaagte hue chulhe

Ik taraf ko gudiya ka
Adh-bana gharaunda thha
Duur ek koney mein
Cycle ka pahiya thha
Murġhiyon ke darbe thhe
Kabukein thhin, pinjra thha
Tees gaz ke aangan mein
Sab hii kuchh to rakkha thha

Eik pal mein ye manzar
Kyun badal sa jaata hai
Ik dhuan sa uthta hai
Haan magar dhundalke mein
Kuchh dikhai deta hai
Jaanamaaz ka kona
Jhaadiyon mein uljha hai
Safha-e-Kalaam-e-Paak
Khaak par larazta hai

Muslim-Muslim Riot

At daybreak, a sight:
A household bustling—
A wife scolding
Children running
Clothes swinging
In the arms of the clothesline
Pots and pans in loud conversation
And hearths awakening.
To a side
A half-built doll-house,
In the far corner
The wheel of a bicycle,
In the hen coop
A few cages and pigeon holes.
Almost everything was present
In that thirty-feet courtyard.

In the flash of an eye
This tableau changes.
Smoke rises,
In the dawning day
Something can be seen:
A corner of a prayer mat
Tangled in the bushes.
A page of the Holy Quran
Trembling in the dust.

Saath aur ḳhabron ke
Ye ḳhabar bhi chhapti hai
Log iss ko padhte hain
Baatein hoti rahti hain
Kaam chalte rahte hain
Ambulance Edhi ki
Bain karti aati hai
Sab jali kati laashein
Saath le ke jaati hai
Subh tak sabhi laashein
Dafn kar di jaati hain
Auraton ki bachchon ki
Boodhon aur jawaanon ki

Masjidon se hoti hain
Baarishein azaanon ki

La 'ilaha 'illa llahu
La 'ilaha 'illa llahu

Along with all the other news
This one too is published.
People read it
And they talk,
Life goes on.
Edhi's ambulance* comes
With its siren blaring,
It carries away
All the burnt and hacked bodies.
By the morning
All the corpses have been buried,
The women and children
The young and old.
From the mosques
There is a shower of the *azaan*:

La 'ilaha 'illa llahu!
La 'ilaha 'illa llahu!†

*The Edhi Foundation is a non-profit humanitarian organization founded by Abdul Sattar Edhii n 1951, headquartered in the city of Karachi. It provides 24-hour emergency assistance across Pakistan and internationally. The foundation provides, among many other services, shelter for the destitute, hospitals and medical care, drug rehabilitation services, and national and international relief efforts, as well as ambulance services.

†The opening part of the *kalmia* (declaration of faith in Islam), it means 'There is no God but Allah'); it goes on to say 'And Muhammad is His prophet').

Eik Phool Sa Bachcha

Eik din thaka-maanda
Eik shaam be-maani
Eik raat hairaan si
Mere saath ye tinon
Mere ghar mein rahte hain
Eik doosre se kum
Apne aap se hum log
Baat karte rahte hain
Uljhe suljhe lamhon ki
Waqt chadarein bun kar
Hum ko dhaanp deta hai
Dekhta nahin murh kar
Jald jald kat-ta hai
Hum jo dekhna chaahein
Vo nazar churaata hai
Eik phuul sa bachcha
Be-ḳhabar nidar sachcha
Mere ghar ke kamron mein
Aa ke ġhul machaata hai
Munjamid ḳhamoshi ko
Todti hansi uss ki
Iss tarah bikharti hai
Jaise thahre paani mein
Koi kankari pheinke
Aks jhuum jhuum utthe
Mauj mauj lahrae
Eik din thaka-maanda
Jaag jaag jaata hai
Eik shaam be-maani
Harf harf sajti hai
Eik raat hairan sii
Aankh muund leti hai

A Flower-Like Child

An exhausted day
A meaningless evening
A bewildered night.
The three of them
Live with me in my house.
We keep talking,
Less with each other and more with ourselves.
Time covers us with blankets
Woven from tangled-untangled moments
And passes by quickly, quickly.
He averts his gaze;
He doesn't turn to look.

A flower-like child
A carefree, fearless child
Enters the rooms in my house
Creates a din
And breaks the frozen silence.
His laughter spreads
As if someone
Has tossed a pebble in still waters;
Like a reflection
That dances and sways
With every ripple and wave.
An exhausted day
Comes to wakefulness
A meaningless evening
Adorns itself with words
A bewildered night
Closes its eyes.

Pul Sirat

Main jis mein rahti huun mera ghar hai
Yahan ki deewar-o-dar ke andar
Miri jawaani ke taane-baane
Har ik rag-e-sang mein ravaan hain
Yahan pe nikhri hui safedi
Mire budhaape ki aane waali
Sehar ka elaan kar rahi hai
Yahan ki chhat mere dil se nikli hui dua hai
Jo bargaah-e-Khuda mein maqbool ho ke saaya kiye hue hai
Yahan ki khidki yahan ke rauzan
Miri hii ankhon ke ḳhwaab hain
Kuchh mein raushni kuchh bujhe bujhe hain

Yahan pe kuchh log rah chuke hain
Yahan pe kuchh log rah rahe hain
Hamaare mabain kya hai maazi ke rabte hain
Vo raabte jin pe sirf meri giraft mahfooz rah gai hai
Jabhi to aisa hua hai aksar
Main apne haathon ko ḳhud jhatak kar
Nikal padi aise raaste par
Jo baal se bhi maheen
Talvaar ki tarah
Tund-o-murtaish thha
Main kat ke gir jaana chaahti thhi
Bikhar ke mar jaana chaahti thhi
Magar na-jaane mujhe hua kya
Bajaaye iss ke ki neeche dekhun
Miri inn aankhon ne peechhe dekha
Wahin jahan ek ghar kharha thha
Vo jis ki khidki vo jis ke rauzan
Miri hii ankhon ke ḳhwaab thhe, kuchh mein raushni,
    kuchh bujhe bujhe the

The Bridge of Sirat*

This is my home
Behind its walls
The warp and weft of my youth
Run through its bricks and mortar.
The silver that is spread here
Announces the dawn
Of my approaching old age.
Its roof is every prayer that emerged from my heart
And has been granted in the court of my God.
The windows and crevices here
Are the dreams my eyes have dreamt,
Some are lit, some snuffed out.

Some people have lived here
Some people are living here
And between us lie bonds of the past,
Those bonds on which I alone have a firm grip anymore.
Which is why it has often happened
That I myself shook my hands free
And set off on a path
That was thinner than a single hair,
Sharp as a sword
Taut and trembling—
I wanted to be gashed, I wanted to fall.
I wanted to scatter, and die.
But I don't know what happened to me,
Instead of looking down
These eyes of mine turned back to look—
There, where stood a house
Whose windows and crevices
Bore the dreams my eyes had dreamt,
Some were lit, some snuffed out.

---

*The bridge of Sirat is, according to Islam, the bridge which every human must pass on the Day of Resurrection to enter Paradise. It is not mentioned in the Quran, but is described in the *Hadith*. As-Sirat is said to be thinner than a strand of hair and as sharp as the sharpest sword; below this path are the fires of Hell which burn the sinners who do not cross the bridge.

Raaste

Ab talak un nigahon mein mahfuz hain
Seedhe-saade vo viran se aaste
Apne hamraaz apne shanaasa
Apne dukh apne sukh donon pahchaante
Oonghte jaagte thhaharte bhaagte
Bheege bheege vo hairan se raaste
Dekhte dekhte ek pul ban gaya
Aur samundar ka paani simat kar samundar se phir mil gaya
Dhoop se tap ke mitti ka giila badan jaag utha tan gaya

Ghar humakne lage, log basne lage
Rang lau de uthe, phool hansne lage
Ab kahin koi tanha sadak koi viran kona ubharta nahin
Koi dildar saaya bulaata nahin, koi ġham-ḳhvaar rasta nikalta nahin

Pathways

They are still safe in those eyes
Those simple, straight, desolate pathways
Confidantes, dearly familiar
Knowing each other's joys and sorrows
Dozing, awakening, pausing, running.
Those wet, somewhat surprised pathways.
In the blink of an eye, a bridge was formed
The waters of the sea shrank, and then returned to the sea,
Baked by the sun, the damp body of the earth woke up, taut,
Houses began to twitch, people began to settle down,
Colours caught fire, flowers began to laugh.
Now, no lonely road or desolate corner can be seen,
No beloved shadow calls out, no sympathetic pathways emerge.

Mashwara

Mujhe ye dar hai kisi aaftab ki garmi
Tiri nazar ke hazaar aainon ko tod naa de
Mujhe ye vahm kisi mahtaab ki thandak
Lahu se garmi-e-fikr-o-amal nichod na le

Tu apni zaat se ḳhud chashma-e-ada-o-sada
Tujhe jahaan ki havaaon ke ruḳh se kya nisbat
Tu apne-aap hii ḳhud anjuman hai ḳhud hii charaġh
Hujuum-e-halqa-ba-goshan se tujh ko kya nisbat
Ye raasta nahin vo jis pe tu thhahar jaae
Yahan se jald guzar aks-e-mehr-o-mah ki tarah
Yahan pe koi ruka hai to ḳhaar-e-rah ki misaal
Yahan pe koi ruka hai to gard-e-rah ki tarah

Jo aastaan ho ussey sang-e-daar ka ġham kaisa
Jo ḳhud safar ho ussey rahguzar ka ġham kaisa
Jo ḳhud yaqin ho ussey vahm-e-intizam se kya
Jo ḳhud hii mai ho ussey mai-kade ke naam se kya

Advice

I'm afraid that the heat of some sun might
Break the thousand mirrors of your glance.
I fear that the coolness of some moon might
Drain the fervour of thought and deed from your blood.

Your very being is the flowing spring of sights and sounds
Why concern yourself with the direction of the world's winds?
You are the congregation by yourself, you are the lamp
Why concern yourself with crowds of devoted slaves?
This is not the path on which you can pause.
Traverse swiftly like the reflection of the sun and the moon.
Those who stop here stop as if halted by a thorn in the path,
Those who stop here stop like the dust raised on the path.

That which is the threshold knows not the sorrow of the stone
of the doorway,
That which is itself the journey knows not the sorrow
of the pathway.
That which is conviction itself, why need it bother with plans
and arrangements?
To that which is itself the wine, how does the name
of the tavern matter?

Sylvia Plath

Deewani thhi ke siyani thhi
Par aurat bari jiyaali thhi
Vo maut ko muth-thi mein pakrey
Iss aan se zinda rahti thhi
Jab chahey muth-thi kholeygi
Mar jayegi...

Sylvia Plath

Maybe she was insane, maybe she was wise,
But she was certainly a brave woman.
Grasping Death in her fist
She lived life with such elan—
She could open her fist any time she wanted
And die.

Eik Barhey Musawwir Ke Naam

Jahaan-e-rang-o-bu me vo barahna pa
Rawaan dawaan hai or dekhta nahi
Ke roz-o-shab ne kitney maah-o-saal ke taano pe bun diye
Palat ke dekhta nahi
Ke barishon se sab imarton ke rang bah gaye
Vo jaanta hai uske rukh ki raushni
Vo subah jaisi dilkashi, abhi talak gudaaz hai
Kisi dhanak ki khoj mein vo saarey mausamon se be-niyaaz thha
Vo saarey mausamon se be-niyaaz thha

To a Great Artist

Walking barefoot in this brightly coloured world
He moves swiftly but doesn't see
How days and nights have woven webs of months and years.
He doesn't turn to see
How the rains have washed away the colours from all the buildings.
He knows the radiance of his face,
Pleasing as the light of the morning, is diffused, gentle.
In search of some rainbow, he was unmindful of all the seasons.
He was unmindful of all the seasons.

Taameel-e-Wafa ka Ahadnaama

Khamosh hain sahibaan-e-munsif
Hairaan hain rahbaraan-e-muḳhlis
Laashon ka koi watan nahin hai
Murdon ki koi zabaan nahin hai
Ujde hue ghar ki ḳhamoshi mein
Nauhe ki nidaein ek sii hain
Maatam ka hai lahja ek jaisa
Roney ki sadaaen ek sii hain
Aankhon ki siyaahiyaan hain maddham
Palkon ki qalam hai paara-paara
Khunaab hua hai mushaf-e-ruḳh
Honton ke haiṇ daaere shikasta
Chehre ki kitaab ke waraq par
Zaḳhmon ne jo haashiye likhe hain
Inn sab ki zabaan hai ek jaisi
Vo sab ki samajh mein aa gaie hai
Ik pal ke liye shab-e-alam mein
Chamkenge tasalliyon ke aansu
Kuchh der darida-daamanon mein
Mahkegi sataishon ki ḳhushboo
Phir ḳhaak ki jild mein chhupega
Taameel-e-wafa ka ahadnaama
Mil jaaengi waarison ko yaadein
Ho jaega qafila rawaana

The Testament of Constancy

The dispensers of justice are silent
The sincerest of guides are puzzled,
There is no country for corpses
The dead have no tongues.
In the silence of a desolate home
Dirges sound the same
The tenor of lamentations is the same
The crying voices are the same
The ink of the eyes is smudged
The quill of the lashes is torn to shreds
The book of the face is bloodied
The rims of the lips are askew.
On the pages of the book of the face
The notes that wounds have written
All speak in the same tongue,
Everyone has understood what they say.
For one moment in the Night of Calamity
The tears of consolation will sparkle,
For a while this tattered hem
Will be fragrant with eulogies;
Then the testament of constancy
Will be hidden between covers of dust,
The heirs will be granted memories
And the caravan will move on.

Hazaaron Abu Jahl

Hazaaron Abu Jahl
Rah-e-firasat pe
Danish ke sandooq
Sar per uthaaye
Chaley aa rahe hain
Rah-guzaaron mein sahmey huwe log
Unke fatwon pe imaan laatey huwe
Unke qadmon mein bichhtey chaley jaa rahey hain

Har Abu Jahl ke haath mein
Aatisheen vo asaa hai
Jiski awaaz dehshat hai
Karb-o-bala hai
Merey mabood tera ye irshaad hai
Ab payambar nahi aayengey
Phir bata
Unko rokeyga kaun?
Aatisheen unkey hathiyaar ab unsey chheenega kaun?

Thousands of Abu Jahls*

Thousands of Abu Jahls
Are walking on the Path of Wisdom
Carrying the Chest of Knowledge on their head.
The scared people on the road
Repose faith in their mischief,
Willingly lay down at their feet.

Every Abu Jahl carries
A flaming staff in his hand
Whose fire-sound spells fear
And trials and tribulations.
O You, whom I worship and adore,
You have commanded
There shall be no more prophets—
Then tell me:
Who will stop them?
Who will snatch their flaming weapons?

---

*Amr ibn Hisham al-Makhzumi, also known as Abu Jahl (literally 'Father of Ignorance'), was one of the Meccan polytheist leaders from the Quraysh known for his opposition towards Prophet Muhammad and the early Muslims in Mecca.

Daro Uss Waqt Se

Har taraf daur-e-faraamoshi hai
Zehn sahma baitha hai kahin
Apney atraaf hifazat ki tanabein gaarhey
Jab koi baat nahin yaad usko
Phir ye dahshat ka sabab kya maani?
Aur hifazat ka junoon kaisa hai?

Daro uss waqt se jab aisa khauf
Jis ke asbaab nahi miltey hain
Zindagaani mein chala aata hai

Rooh wijdaan bhatak jaati hai
Tarz-e-afkaar badal jaati hai
Aasmanon ke waraq khultey hain
Jauq-dar-jauq parey hooron ke
Chaltey phirtey nazar aa jaatey hain
Aur zameen kaanch ke tukrhon ki tarah toot-ti hai

Weham tasveer mein dhal jaata hai
Kam nigaahi ka tasallut chup-chaap
Duur-andeshi ko khaa jaata hai
Daro uss waqt se jab aisa khauf
Zindagaani mein chala aata hai
Jis ke asbaab nahin miltey hain

Be Fearful of That Time

Spread all around is an Age of Oblivion.
Fearful, the mind is crouching somewhere
Having dug the tent-pegs of security on all sides.
But when it remembers nothing
What is the reason for this terror?
And why this obsession with safety?

Be fearful of that time when this fear
Whose reasons cannot be found
Enters your life—

The spirit of ecstasy loses its way,
The manner of thinking changes,
The leaves of the sky open up
And mobs upon mobs of houris
Can be seen walking about
And the earth cracks like splintered glass.
Superstition is poured into pictures,
The absolute sway of short-sightedness
Silently eats away at far-sightedness.

Be fearful of that time when this fear
Whose reasons cannot be found
Seeps into your life.

Nazm

'Aur phir zinda gaarhi jaaney wali larkiyan tum se apna hisaab mangeingi, ke aakhir unka qusoor kya thaa'

—Qu'an, Surah 81, at-Takwir, 8-9

'Dil darya samandaron doonge kaun dilan diyan jaane hoo'

Beti:
Maae ni...
Marney se pahle mujh ko eik jawaab chaahiye
Merey paas samey thoda hai, phir bhi mujh ko hisaab chaahiye

Baaba ne jab taar ka phanda diya galey me daal
Maine apne hathon se khud todna chaaha jaal

Tu kyun dhoond ke rassi lai, kyun bandhey mere haath
Baaba ko to yeh karna thaa, tu to aurat zaat...

Maae ni marney se pahle mujh ko eik jawaab chaahiye
Merey paas samey thoda hai, phir bhi mujh ko hisaab chaahiye

Maa:
Dhiyye ni...
Sunna chahey to sun ley mera jawaab
Lena chahey to le le mera hisaab

Dhiyye ni...
Jo main terey phande, tere haathon beech me na aati
Phir to tujh ko martey martey badi deir lag jaati

Sisak sisak kar marney se jaldi mar jaana achcha
Aisey hii jaana thhehrey to jaldi jaana achcha

Haath ki rassi kangan terey, galey ka phanda haar
Babul tera dil darya-o, bada hi izzat daar

A Poem

'And then the girl-child being buried alive will ask for what offence was she killed.'

—The Holy Quran, Surah 81, at-Takwir, 8-9

'Dil darya samandaron doonge kaun dilan diyan jaane hoo.'
(The heart is deeper than the ocean, who can fathom its mysteries?)
—Sultan Bahu, 17th-century poet of Punjab

Daughter:
'O mother mine
I need an answer before I die,
I have little time but I want a full account.
When father put a cord around my throat
I tried to break free from the noose.

Why did you bring the rope, why did you tie my hands?
Father had to do it, but you after all are a woman.

I need an answer before I die,
I have little time but I want a full account.'

Mother:
'O daughter mine
If you really want to hear my answer
If you really want to take my account, then:

O daughter mine
Had I not tied your hands together
It would have taken long for you to die.

It is better to die quickly than to linger on,
If one has to go it is better to go quickly.

The ropes on your wrists were bracelets, the noose a necklace.
Your father's heart is an ocean; he is an honourable man.

Terey paas samey thooda hai, doli laye kahaar
Aa main band karoon teri aankhein, saajan kharhey dwaar

You have little time; the bearers have brought your palanquin.
Come, let me close your eyes, your beloved stands at the door.

Eik Muntashir Sii Nazm

Bahut din se tabeeyat muntashir hai, magar kyun hai
Agar ye ilm ho jaata to sab kuchh theek ho jaata
Main apne aap se uktaa gai huun
Theek hai
Aisa bhi hota hai

Main apne kaam se bhi thak gai huun
Yehi likhna likhaana aur kya?
Ab dil nahi lagta...

Mere haathon mein aakar sab kitaabein rooth jaati hain
Mazameen munh chhipate hain
Qalam, kaaghaz, siyahi, sab mujhe aankhein dikhaate hain
Chalo koshish karuun eik aakhiri koshish

Guzishta raat eik khwaab-e-pareshaan maine dekha thha
Usey manzoom kar daluun
Kahaan se ibtidaa ho? Kaheen se bhi
Bhala khwaab-e-pareshaan ki koi tamheed hoti hai

Bahut sii nazmein be-aaghaaz bhi to likhi jaati hain
Magar main duur kyun jaaoon?
Main apne sheher hii se nazm ka aghaaz karti huun
Jahaan rahtii huun main ye sheher mera sheher-e-ghurbat hai
Dikhai go nahi deita
Aik arsey se kai haakim hukumat karney aatey hain
Bahut daulat kamaatey hain
Bahut be-aabru hotey hain
Waapas laut jatey hain
Ameeron ke qabeelon mein haqeeqat aur badhti hai
Ghareebon ke hujoom be-nawa ko khwaab miltey hain

A Distracted Poem

(Note: This translation is an extract from a long poem.)

For many days now I have been distracted. But why?
If I knew why, everything would have been all right.

I'm weary of myself.
It is all right
It happens.

I'm tired of my work too,
The same old reading and writing, what else?
My heart is not in it...

Books become fretful when they come into my hands,
Articles and essays hide their face,
Pen, paper, ink, everything glares angrily at me.

Come, let me try. A last attempt.

Last night I had a troubled dream.
Shall I pour it into verse?
Where shall I begin? It doesn't matter where,
After all, a troubled dream has no preamble,
Many poems are written without a beginning.
But why should I go far,
I shall begin my poem from my own city.
This city where I live is my city of destitution
Even though it doesn't seem so.
For years, many rulers have come to rule it,
They amass wealth
They lose honour and repute
And they go back.
Reality becomes stronger in the tribes of the rich;
The crowds of the indigent receive dreams.

Magar ye baat jo main likh rahi huun
Aisey pahley bhi likhti aai huun shayad
Ussey merey kai hum-asr shair likhtey rahtey hain
Kahi baaton ko phir dohrao ye achcha nahi lagta hai
Suna hai umr badh jaye to baaton ka tasalsul toot jaata hai
Jo qissa kahney baithein, uske daaman se
Naye qissey ulajhtey hain
Sunaana chahtey hain jo, ussi ko bhool jatey hain

Ye dekho!
Main apne khwaab ko manzoom karney jaa rahi thhi...

Guzishta shab ye dekha thha
Hamaare sheher mein eik shor barpa thha
Nai naamon ki takhtee lag rahi hai chawk mein...
Aur shahraahon par...
Hamaarey log mahv-e-raqs hain zo'm hifazat mein
Vo saarey mast hain eik sheher-e-wahsat mein
Mithaai bat rahi hai
Jo ke har mauqe pe bat-ti hai

Koi phaansi pe charh jaye
To laddu baant-te hain hum
Koi be-aabru ho kar chaley jaaye
To bhangra nach-te hain hum
Vohi phir waapas aa jaye
To laddi daaltey hain hum
Koi peechey se aakar takht ka haqdaar ho jaye
"Dil maa-shaad"* kah kar uska kaha maantey hain hum
Bhala iss khwaab ka inn harkaton se kya taalluq hai?
Ye kahna chahti thhi main...

---

*The expressions 'Chashm-e-maa-raushan dil-e-maa-shaad" means "We are/ I am happy" used as an expression of welcome or agreement like saying: You are most welcome!

But this matter that I am writing now,
I have written this before,
Many poets among my peers have written about it too.
It isn't good to repeat what has been said before.
It is said that the flow of words breaks as one ages,
As one sits down to tell stories
New stories get entangled in one's hem
And one forgets what one wants to say—

See!
Here I was, wanting to pour my dream into verse...

In my dream last night
I saw a clamour in my city:
New name plates are being affixed in the city squares
And on the thoroughfares
Our people are engrossed in dance thinking they are safe,
They are frenzied in this city of dread,
Sweets are being distributed
As are often distributed on such occasions—

We distribute laddus
When someone is sent to the gallows,
We dance the bhangra
When someone is sent away in disgrace
And when they come back
We shower them with affection.
And when someone appears to stake a claim to the throne
We obey him and welcome him...

But I wanted to say:
After all, what is the connection between my dream and these realities?

Ijazat Lein

Aao hum bhi ijazat talab karkey uthein
Ijazat lein dereena khwaabon ke deewaar-o-dar se
Jinki thandak se muddat tak aankhein gulistaan rahi hain
Aaj uskey khandar itne veeran hain
Jin mein ek doosre ko pukaro to aawaaz bhi palat-ti nahi hai

Ijazat lein
Waadon ki unn konplon se
Jo ab tak rag-e-jaan mein paiwast thheen
Jo jigar ki tarawish si phailein barhein
Aur darakhton ki surat mein saaya kiye apney humraah thheen
Aaj yun kirm khurda hain jin mein
Parindey bhi ghabra-ke ruktey nahin hain

Ijazat lein
Unn rishtey naaton ki zanjeer se
Jisey paon mein baandh-kar, baazuon mein samo kar
Hamesha fakhr se humney duniya ko dekha
Ab ye hum se gurezan hain or apne halqey
Kisi aur ko sonpna chahti hain

Aao hum bhi ijazat talab kar-ke uthein
Ijazat lein unn se
Jisey humnein chaaha
Aur itna ke khud se, khudai se, apney khuda se zyaada...
Kahin rishta-e-jaan zamaan-o-makaan ki bhanwar mein
Apni zaat or apni ana ko sambhaaley raha hai
Magar ab ye thak gaya hai—
Ijazat lein uss se
Jisey humney chaaha

Taking Leave

Come, let us also take our leave and rise...
Let us take leave of the walls and niches of long-held dreams
Whose coolness for long turned our eyes into flower gardens.
Today their ruins are so desolate
That when we call out to each other even our voices do not echo.

Let us take leave
Of the buds of those promises
That were stuck to our jugular,
That grew and unfurled with the heart's blood
And like shade-giving trees were our companions once
But are now so worm-eaten
That even birds do not stop by.

Let us take leave
Of the chains of relationships
That we had tied around our feet and cradled in our arms
And looked upon the world always with pride.
Now these chains are slipping from us
And want to bestow their shackles upon others.

Come, let us also take our leave and rise...
Let us take leave
Of the one we loved
More than our self, providence and even our God.
In the whirlpool of life and circumstance
That love of our life has been holding safe his self and his dignity
But he is tired now.

Let us take leave
Of the one we loved...

Samandar Isi Jagah Par Thha

Samandar isi jagah par thha
Ghussela, tand-khu, sar paththaron se maarta
Garajta, daurhta, chinghaarhta, taaqat per itraata
Samandar isi jagah par thha
Yahan ke aasmaan ka kam-sukhan maahtaab
Uskey saath chalta thha
Samandar apney baahon mein usey leney ki khaatir
Kis tarah betaab rahta thha
Magar ab kuchh nahi baaqi
Nishaan se rah gaye khaali
Khameeda jism chattaanein
Zabaanein pyaas se baahar
Libaas-e-aab ke kuch malgajjey tukrey
Kisi veeran sahil par
Magar vo dost ab tak bawafa hai
Vo apna aks ab bhi malgajjey tukron pe rakh-kar dekh leta hai

The Sea Was in the Same Place

The sea was in the same place
Fierce, fretful, smashing its head against the rocks
Roaring, running, rumbling, proud of its power.
The sea was in the same place,
The taciturn moon moved along
The sky above
How eager the sea was
To take the sky in its arms!
But nothing remains anymore
Save a few signs:
Some rocks with bent bodies,
Their tongues lolling with hunger,
Wearing a few tattered old garments of water
On a desolate shore.
But that friend is still faithful,
He still sees the reflection
In those tattered old fragments.

Thakaan

Kahan ki thakaan hai?
Ye kaisi thakaan hai?
Dabey paun shahr-e-badan mein ye utri
Ragon mein lahu ki tarah bah rahi hai

Ungliyan bhaar-e-nakhoon se bezaar hain
Meri aankhon pe palkey giraan baar hain
Saans seeney mein masroof-e-aazaar hai
Merey shaanon pe rakh-kha hua baanjh sar
Baar-e-bekaar hai
Ye thakaan qurbaton ki nihayat nahin
Jismey aasoodgi ki mehak ho
Ye thakaan raaston ki musafat nahi
Roo-e-manzil ki jismey jhalak ho

Ye thakaan soch ki bhi alamat nahin
Jis se auron ko koi bashaarat miley
Ye thakaan umar bhar ki alamat nahin
Jis se auron ko jeeney ki himmat miley

Ye thakaan merey andar ki apni thakan
Meri kokh mein palney wali thakaan
Ragon mein lahu ki tarah bah rahi hai
Kahan ki thakaan hai?
Ye kaisi thakaan hai?

Exhaustion

What is this exhaustion?
Where has it come from?
Entering the city of the body on tiptoe
It flows in the veins like blood.

Fingers weary with the weight of nails
Lashes weighing down my eyes
Breaths busy tormenting my chest
On my shoulders the useless burden of a barren head.

This exhaustion is not brought on by the intimacy
Of relationships redolent with the fragrance of contentment;
This exhaustion is not the friend of those roads
That offer a glimpse of the face of the destination;
This exhaustion is not even the sign of deep thinking
That might bring some revelation to others;
Nor is it the token of a long life
That might lend courage to others to stay alive.

This exhaustion is my own inner fatigue.
The exhaustion nurtured in my womb,
Flowing like blood in my veins.

What is this exhaustion?
Where has it come from?

Mujhe Fursat Hii Fursat Hai

Mujhe fursat hii fursat hai
Saverey jald uthna hai
Na shab der se sona
Kahiin baahar nahin jaana
Kisi se bhi nahin milna
Na koi fikr laahaq hai
Na koi yaad baaqi hai

Magar ye aakhiri misra
Zara sa jhoot lagta hai

I Have All the Time in the World

I have all the time in the world.
I don't have to get up early in the morning
Nor sleep late at night
I don't have to go out anywhere
Nor meet any one at all
I have no worries troubling me
Nor any memories left—

Only this last line
Seems a little false.

Rishtey

Yeh risthey
Azal se abad tak ke rishtey
Khwahison ki namu jin ki buniyaad thhe
Jin se duniya-e-dil bargaah-e-nazar kaisi aabaad thhi

Ye saanson ki tarah
Rag-e-jaan se peiwast rishtey
Azal se abad tak ke rishtey

Jab ye tootey
Samandar bhi saakit raha
Pahaarh apni waza pe qaaim rahey
Zameenein bhi sotii rahin
Kuchh hua hii nahi

Inka anjaam aisey hua jaisey aaghaaz thha hii nahin

Relationships

These relationships
That stretch from eternity to endless time,
Their foundation was the world of desires
They lit up my heart's world, the vistas before my eyes.

Like my breaths
They were entwined with my veins,
These relationships that stretch from eternity to endless time.

When they ended,
The sea stood still
The mountains remained in their place
The earth slumbered on
Nothing happened at all.

They ended as though they had never begun.

Eik Kahaani Bahut Puraani

Baarish laaney wala devta
Indr
Eik basti se khafa thha
Uss basti ke rahney waley
Eik eik kar-key martey jaatey
Pyaasey chatkhey maidanon mein
Unke pinjar sookhtey jaatey

Indr ne eik din yon socha
Uss basti mein ghoomney jayein
Apni khaftgi ki taaqat ka
Jaakar andaaza to lagayein
Indr uss basti mein aaya
Dekh ke uss basti ki haalat
Apni quwwat par itraaya
Jaatey jaatey usney dekha
Eik johar gadla gadla sa
Jis-ke paas eik bhoori chirhya
Baithii hui thhi
Dhoondh dhoondh ker eik eik qatra
Apni chonch mein bhar letii thhi
Sookhey khet pe daal aati thhi
Haanp rahi thhi
Kaanp rahi thhi
Lekin kaam kiye jaati thhi
Indr ne chirhya ko dekha
Khoob hansa or uss-se bola:
'Murakh! Teri iss mehnat se
Sookha khet hara nahi hoga
Teri iss eik boond se, paagal
Koi dukh achcha nahi hoga'

An Old, Old Story

The God who brings rain,
Indra
Was once angry with a village
The people who stayed there
Died one by one,
Their skeletons dried up
In thirsty, cracked fields.

One day Indra thought
Of going to visit that village
To at least get a sense
Of the power of his wrath.
Indra went to that village
He saw its condition
And preened at his might.
As he was leaving, he saw
A somewhat muddied pond
And a little brown bird
Sitting beside it
Searching for water.
It would fill its beak drop by drop
And shower it over the parched field.
It was puffing and panting
It was shivering and quivering
Yet it carried on working.

Indra looked at the bird
Laughed loudly and said:
'You foolish bird! The dry field
Will not turn green with your labour,
With this one drop, you idiot,
The sorrows will not go away.'

Chirhya bhi Indr devta par
Khoob hansi or hans ke boli:
'Tu taaqat ke zor mein apney
Saarey faraiz bhool gaya hai
Aur main qehat ki dhoop mein ab tak
Apna farz nahin bhooli hoon
Main matyaili rangat wali
Be-bas chirhya
Apna kaam kiye jaati hoon
Apna kaam kiye jaungi
Taakey tujh ko ghairat aaye'

The bird too laughed loudly at Indra
And said:
'You have forgotten your duties
Blinded as you are by your strength.
But I have not forgotten my duty.
In the blinding glare of this famine
I, a mud-coloured
Helpless little bird,
Continue to do my work,
I shall continue to do my work
So that you might know some shame.'

Billi

Dabey paon chalti chali aayegi
Kisi garm koney mein chupkey se baitheygi
Billori aankhein ghumaati rahegi
Kabhi eik halki jamaai bhi legi
Dekhtey dekhtey jism se uthney wali mehak
Saarey kamrey mein bhar jayegi

Dayaar-e-ghareeban se aaya hua eik adherh umr chooha
Jo bas rizq ki bu ko pahchaanta hai
Jo har waqt bimaar, har waqt bezaar chuhiyya se tang aa chuka hai
Usse dekh lega to jee jayega
Shauq-e-waraftgi, tarz-e-aamaadgi
Usko billi ke nazdeek le jaayega
Lamha-e-qurb mein
Saa.at-e-wasl mein
Uss haseena ke nakhoon nikal aayeingey
Issi adherh choohey se shokhi kareingey
Usse haanpta kaanpta adh-mara chorh kar
Phir se malboos makhmal mein chhup jaayeingey

Cat

Soft-footed, she pads in
To sit quietly in some warm corner
Rolling her tawny eyes
She might also yawn delicately, occasionally
Within a matter of moments
The scent from her body will fill the room.

A middle-aged mouse will come in from outside
He only recognises the scent of food
He is tired of his forever ailing, forever listless wife
He will see the cat and perk up
A mad desire, a willingness to surrender
Will take him towards the cat
In this moment of closeness
In this instant of meeting
That beauty's talons will appear
They will tease that middle-aged rat
Leaving him panting and half dead,
Then retreat into their velvety furriness.

Parindey Ijtimaa-e-Khwaab Ke Sahra Mein Urhtey Hain

Parindey ijtimaa-e-khwaab ke sahra mein urhtey hain
Jab aankhein band hon to simt kaisi, raastey kaisey?
Thakan se dono baazu shal hain
Aur par jharhtey jaatey hain
Zara si duur jaakar aag ka dariya milega
Gir parheingey, khaak hongey
Phir inkey khwaab ka ghaul bayabaan
Khas-o-khashaak mein tabeer apni dekh lega
Bas eik kiran talak hai jeena
Ye jaan ke gir rahi hai shabnam

Birds Fly in the Wilderness of Collective Dreams

Birds fly in the wilderness of collective dreams
When the eyes are shut, rows and paths don't matter.
Wings heavy with fatigue,
Shedding feathers along the way,
Shortly they will come to a river of fire.
They will fall in it, turn to ashes.
Then the wild ghoul of their dreams
Will see the interpretation of his dreams in sticks and straws.

The dew falls
Knowing that it will stay alive till the first ray of the sun.

Coma

Manzar 1
Meri suniye
To mat miliye
Hamari maa hain lekin
Ab nahi pehchaanti humko
Mualij, dost, rishtedaar
Himmat haar baithey hain…
Magar aap unko kaisey jaantey hain? Ye to batlayein
Larhakpan mein parhosi rah chukey hain aap?
To phir aaiyye andar…
Issi daalaan ke daayein taraf
Vo unka kamra hai
Vahaan par nurse baithi hai
Ussi se saara haal pooch lijiyega
Maafi chahtey hain hum…
Zara jaldi mein hain, humko kisi daawat mein jaana hai

Manzar 2
Suniye, sister!
Kabhi ye apni aankhein kholti bhi hain?
Kabhi kuchh bolti bhi hain?

Nahi, sahab
Mukammal taur per ghaayab hain ye gyaarah maheenon se
Yehi eik dhoonkni hai saans ki jo chalti rahti hai
Ye taar zindagi ab toot hi jaye to behtar hai
Na jaaney kis tarah ye seedhi muththi band kar li hai
Bahut koshish kii sabne, par nateeja kuchh nahin nikla
Mujhey lagta hai inki jaan hai iss band muththi mein

Coma

Scene 1
If you ask me
It's best not to meet her
She's our mother
But she doesn't recognise us.
Family, friends, relatives,
Everyone has given up...
But how do you know her, please tell us.
You were neighbours when you were both young?
All right then, come in...
On the right side of this verandah
There, that is her room.
A nurse is sitting there
You can ask her the details...
I'm sorry...
I'm in a bit of a hurry; I have to go for a dinner

Scene 2
Listen sister
Does she ever open her eyes?
Does she ever say anything?

No, sir
She's been gone completely for eleven months now
Only the bellows of her breath work;
Though it'd be better if this string of life were to snap...
No one knows how she has clenched her right fist so tightly,
Everyone has tried to open it, to no avail.
I feel her life is clenched within it.

Manzar 3

Vo apna thar-tharata haath uss muththi pe rakhta hai
Aur eik namkeen qatra, band muththi par tapakta hai
Hawas-e-khamsa ke sakit samandar par kahin lehar uthti hai
Larazti ungliyaan eik doosrey se baat karti hain
Ulajhti saans ki awaaz madh-dham hoti jaati hai
Vo muththi khulti jaati hai

Scene 3

He places his trembling hand on that clenched fist
And a salty drop falls on the closed hand.
A wave rises somewhere in the still ocean of the five senses
Trembling fingers talk to each other,
The sound of tangled breathing slows
As the closed fist loosens and opens.

Ijlaas

Aabnoosi mez
Uskey ird-gird
Sahibaan-e-feham
Sar jorhey huwe
Saamney phoolon ke guldastey
Rupehla saaf paani botlon mein
Aur billauriin gilaas
Taakey lab ki tishnagi
Taqreer mein haail na ho
Faisla karna hai unko jabr ka aur qadr ka
Aman ke paighambar
Aashti ke thekedaar
Maalik-e-hosh-o-hawaas

Derh ghantey tak raha ijlaas
Cameron ki raushni jalti rahi bujhti rahi
Aur akhbaron ko surkhi mil gai
Guftugu chalti rahi
Sahibaan-e-feham aakhir thak gaye
Aaqilaan-e-deher uththey
Apney apney mashwaron ko saath le kar
Apney apney hotlon mein so gaye
Eik poora shehar sholon mein nahaata hi raha
Eik ghaflat aag mein jalti rahi

Meeting

An ebony table
And seated around it
Men of intellect
With their heads together.
In front of them bouquets of flowers
And sparkling water in glass bottles
And crystal glasses
So that the thirst on their lips
Is not reflected in their speech.
They have to pronounce a verdict on force and merit,
These prophets of peace
These upholders of reconciliation
These powers that be.

The confabulations lasted an hour and a half.
The cameras flashed on and off.
The newspapers got their headlines.
The talks continued.
The men of intellect finally tired
And went to sleep in their hotel rooms,
Carrying their suggestions,
While an entire city bathed in live embers
An entire populace burnt to cinders.

Aik Sipahi Ke Naam
(Jiske Muqaddar Mein Apni Sarhadon Pe Larhna Nahi Hai)

Jaaney wala apni raah pe jaaney ko tayyar hai
Hathiyaaron se badan saja hai
Sar par lohey ki topi hai
Kandhey par khaaki thaila hai
Thaila kya hai?
Jadoo ki zambeel hi samjho...
Jis mein uski saari duniya dosh badosh chali aai hai
Pichley jaarhey boorhi maa ne bun kar eik mufflar bhejaa thha
Vo bhi simat kar eik koney mein baith gaya hai
Coffee ke matiyailey mug par bachchon ki tasweer chhapi hai
Vo bhi aik silwat se nikal kar jhaank rahi hai
Biwi ki palkon ke sitaarey
Thailey ki andhyaari raat mein chamak rahey hain
Thorhi dair mein shaaney ki deewaar giregi
Saji sajaai jadoo nagri mar jayegi
Eik eik cheez bikhar jayegi
Phir eik badsoorat tayyara
Dosh-e-hawa pe shor machata
Chashm-e-falaq se aankh larhaata
Aag ugalta dhuaan urhaata
Seena-e-arz ko zakhmi karta
Aa jayega
Apni andhi kokh se eik kaala taboot janam dega
Biwi ki palkon ke sitaarey
Qaumi parcham par lahraatey
Uss taboot se liptey hongey
Hum sab sochtey rah jayeingey
Ghar ko chhorh kar sehra sehra kaahe ko hairaan hua vo
Kis ke liye qurbaan hua vo!

To a Soldier
(Who is Not Destined to Fight on the Borders of His Country)

He who must go is standing, ready to leave,
His body adorned with arms and ammunitions
An iron helmet on his head
A khaki haversack slung from his shoulder.
And not an ordinary haversack...
You could say it's a magical bag
Containing his entire world:
The muffler his old mother had knitted for him last winter
Has gathered itself into one corner,
The grubby coffee mug with his children's photograph on it
Peers from the bag,
The stars of his wife's eyelashes
Glimmer in the black night of the bag.
In a little while
It will fall from his shoulder,
Everything will scatter
As an ugly aircraft
Will appear
Screaming through the air
Cocking a snook at the skies
Spewing fire, spitting smoke
Wounding the breast of the earth
It will birth a black coffin from its blind womb.
The stars of the wife's eyes
Will spangle on the national flag
Draped over the coffin.
The rest of us will be left to wonder:
Why did he travel to this distant wasteland
Leaving his home behind?
For whom did he martyr himself?

Khwaab-e-Firdaus-e-Bareen

Ye khabar aai ke uska sir mila
Sar ki paimaish hui
Phir zakhm doozi ki gai
Aur ye andaaza hua
Marney wala naujaawan thha
Umar kya thhi?
Bas yehi aththara saal
Zindagi karney ko kul aththara saal?
Parda-e-TV pe bhi sar ki numaish hui
Dekhney walon ne dekha
Eik wahshat ka samaan
Dahshaton ki dastaan

Adhkhuli eik aankh
Jis me khwaab thha uljha hua
Khoon mein lithrha hua
Khwaab-e-firdaus-e-bareen
Doodh ki aur shehad ki nehrein rawaan
Muntazir hoorein kunwaari dil-nasheen
Khosha angoor thhaamey
Sab ke sab masnad nasheen

Sar ki peshaani sili to phir nazar aaya hamein
Sajda rezi ke nishaan
Dayein jaanib chalney walon ka ilm
Madah jinki safah-e-Quran par tahreer hai
Roz-e-mehshar raushni jiski ayaan
Ai Khuda, Ai Qadir-e-Mutlaq Khuda
Apney deen ki aabroo mahfooz rakh
Kis ada se ho rahi hai aaj takmeel-e-jihaad
Jazba-e-shauq-e-shahaadat kis tarah pamaal hai?

Dream of the Highest Paradise

The news came that his head had been found.
It was measured
The wounds were examined
And it was surmised
The dead man must have been young.
How old?
No more than eighteen.
Only eighteen years to the end of a life?
The head was displayed on television,
The viewers saw
A horrifying spectacle
A story of horrors.

In the partly open eye
A tangled dream—
Swaddled though it was in blood—
Of the highest paradise, where
Streams of milk and honey run
Houris stand by, nubile and beautiful,
Holding bunches of grapes
While everyone is ensconced on thrones.

An examination of the forehead showed
The imprint of prostrations,
The mark of those who walk on the right side,
Whose praise is inscribed on the pages of the Quran
Whose light will shine forth on the Day of Judgement.

O God, O Omnipotent One,
Keep the honour of my country safe.
Look, how jihad is being waged.
Look, how the zeal for martyrdom is being disgraced.

Eik Tasweer

Raat gaye eik tasweer
Bolney waaley sandooqon ke chehrey par thhi
Subah sawerey akhbaaron ki peshaani pe utar aai thhi
Phir to ghar ka kona kona uss tasweer se bhara hua thha
Maine uss-se nazar bacha-kar aasmaan ko dekhna chaaha

Hadd-e-nazar tak neela ambar uss tasweer se dhaka hua thha

Uss tasweer mein do shaffaaf barahna tan thhe
Taish-e nau-umari se tarshey
Shor machaati zinda sarhak par
Uljhe suljhe parhey hue thhe
Khud bhi thorhey bahut zinda thhe
Unke galon se chamrhey ki zanjeer bandhi thhi
Sar par eik dilaawar aurat uss zanjeer ko thhamey hue thhi
Muththi ki sakhti se ragon ka jaal tana thha
Hadd-e-nazar tak neela ambar uss tasweer se dhaka hua thha

Soch rahi huun:
Ye aurat to uss tahzeeb ki parwarda hai
Jis mein raah-e-mohabbat ki pahli manzil hi yahi badan hai
Shayad inn poron se ussney
Kisi rida-e-badan ke dhaagey
Dheerey dheerey suljhaye hon
Shayad ussney inn baanhon ke haar kisi ko pahnaaye hon
Inn haathon par ahad-e-wafa ka
Gahrey neeley rang ka phool khila ho
Innhi ragon ne kokh mein palney waaley ko sairaab kiya ho
Yeh takreem jism se be-behra aurat kaisi aurat hai?
Yeh tazeem badan se na-waaqif aurat kaisi aurat hai?
Ahkaamat pe izzat ke saudey to bahut hotey dekhey hain
Aurat apni fitrat beichey
Shayad pahli baar hua hai

An Image*

Till late in the night
A picture was splashed on the 'talking boxes'.
By morning it was smeared on the forehead of the newspapers.
Soon every corner of the house was filled with it.
I tried to look away and look at the sky instead
But even the blue sky stretching as far as the eye could see
   was covered with the picture.

Two naked bodies were clearly visible in that image
Carved out of youthfulness, they
Lay sprawled upon a bustling road
And seemed only partly alive.
A leather leash was tied around each neck.
A bold woman held the leashes so tightly
The veins in her fist stood out.
Even the blue sky stretching as far as the eye could see
   was covered with the picture.

And I think:
This woman is a product of a culture in which
The very first stage on the path of love is the body;
Perhaps with these very fingertips
She might have slowly disentangled the threads of this body.
She might have wound these arms around someone's neck.
Perhaps the flower of constancy
Had once bloomed on these hands.
These very veins might have nurtured a life in her womb.
And now bereft of the slightest respect for the body,
What sort of woman is this?
Unmindful of any reverence for the body,
What sort of woman is this?
We have seen the sale of honour upon the orders of others,
But for a woman to sell her very nature—
Perhaps this is the first time that has happened.

---

*In 2004, images of torture from Abu Ghraib shocked the world. Lyndie England, an American soldier, was shown dragging naked prisoners around with leashes around their necks.

Phir Eik Baar Yun Hua

Phir eik baar yun hua
Ke aasmaan phat gaya
Aur zameen jhulas gayi
Pahaarh reiza reiza ban ke urh gaye
Samandaron ki saans ruk gai
Tamam jinn-o-ins
Sab charind
Sab parind
Eik jami hui fiza mein qaid ho ke barf ho gaye
Ussi gharhi nikal parha
Paanch saat jheengron ka qaafila
Zameen ki bachi khuchi tahon ko chat-ta
Jami hui fiza ko kaat-ta hua

Khaar-daar baahein unki jhoomti
Laal laal aankhein unki ghoomti
Moonchhein taan taan ke
Eik niraali shaan se
Seetiyaan baja baja ke chheekhtey:
'Ai sukoot-e-waqt toot
Hum se kuch kalaam kar
Ai minar-e-fana
Jhuk kar humein salaam kar
Hum hii yadgaar hain
Naaib-e-Khuda ke ilm-o-fazl ki
Ab hamaarey haath mein jahaan ka intizaam hai
Bas hameen dawaam hai
Bas hameen dawaam hai...'

And It So Happened One Day

And it so happened one day
The sky split open
The earth was singed
The mountains broke into motes and flew away
To fall into the seas
The seas were choked
All spirits and men
All the beasts
All the birds
Were caged in a prison of ice.

At that very moment
A caravan of five or six crickets set out,
Licking what remained of the earth,
Cutting through the frozen air.

Their scaly limbs moved
Their red eyes rolled
Their antennae twitched
As they screamed:
'Break, O Silence of Time!
Talk to us
O Minaret of Mortality!
Bow down, greet us
We are the reminders
Of Man's wisdom and grace.
We hold the reins of the world.
Only we are eternal
Only we are eternal...'

Maazi aur Haal

Maazi
Do bachche apne kamre se
Taaron vaale kapde pahne
Mere kamre mein aate hain
Mujh se lipat kar so jaate hain
Aur meri be-ḳhwaab aankhon mein
Neend ki thandak bhar jaati hai

Haal
Ghar ki biwi
Apni aaya se kahti hai
Raat gae mere donon bachche
Kyun mere kamre mein aate hain?
Mujh se lipat kar so jaate hain
Tum aaḳhir kaahe ke liye ho?
Meri ḳhwaab-aalud ankhon se
Saari neend bikhar jaati hai

Past and Present

Past
Dressed in star spangled clothes
Two children come from their room
Enter my bedroom
Cling to me and fall asleep
And the coolness of sleep
Suffuses my dreamless eyes.

Present
The lady of the house
Tells the ayah:
'Why do both my children
Come into my room at night
To cling to me and sleep—
After all, why are you here?'
And all the sleep falls away
From my dream-filled eyes.

Pursa
(Simone de Beauvoir ke Naam—Sartre ki Maut Par)

Vo terey saath thha, na thha
Jawaab iska kaun dey
Magar tu usske saat thhi
Ye qurb bhi ajeeb thha
Na koi tamgha-e-wafa
Na koi muhar-e-bandagi
Bas ek ahad-e-zindagi
Vo laal-e-shab chiragh thha
Tu usska haath thhaam kar
Barhi to iss tarah barhi
Hawain ba-adab huin
Bipharney waale mausamon
Ne raastey bana diye
Hazaar gul bichha diye
Chiraagh raushni ka zar bikherta chala gaya
Jahaan jagmaga utha
Vo raushni terey ruwein ruwein mein jazb ho gai
Iss iktisaab-e-zar se tera jism jal gaya

Condolence: To Simone de Beauvoir, on Sartre's Death

Was he with you or was he not
Who can answer this question?
But you were with him.
This proximity was strange:
No medal of loyalty,
No stamp of service,
Simply an age lived together.
He was the ruby that shone like a lamp in the night;
Holding his hand
You surged forward.
The winds bowed respectfully,
The angry seasons
Smoothed the way for you,
Strewed flowers in your path.
The lamp spread the gold of his light,
The world glimmered in its glow,
Every pore of your body absorbed the light
And your body burnt in its gold.

Puraana Shajar

Raat toofaan mein eik shajar gir parha
Vo puraana shajar eik muddat se patton
se mahroom thha
Uski be-chain rooh shaakhon se tang aake
Saarey parindey hawa ho chukey thhe
Uskey be-rang chehrey se ukta ke
Saarey hii mausam sada ho chukey thhe
Phir bhi kal raat jab vo gira
Shakhsaaron par baithe hue
Aashiyanon mein soye hue
Aur hawaon mein urhtey hue
Uske sarey parindon ke dil thham gaye
Rang faq ho gaye
Seeney shaq ho gaye
Unn parindon ki hairaan aankhon ne dekha
Uss puraane shajar ki to saari jarhein unke
seenon se nikli hui hain

An Old Tree

Last night a tree came down in the storm.
For long, the old tree had been bereft of leaves.
Tired of its lifeless branches
All the birds had flown away,
Tired of its colourless visage
All the seasons had gone away.
Yet, when it fell last night
All the birds sitting on other branches
Or sleeping in their nests
Or flying in the air
Held their breath
And went pale.
They were astounded
To see
The tangled roots of the old tree
Emerging from their hearts.

II
Ghazal

Eik ke Ghar ki Khidmat ki...

Eik ke ghar ki ḳhidmat ki aur eik se dil se mohabbat ki
Donon farz nibha kar uss ne saari umr ibadat ki

Dast-e-talab kuchh aur badhaate haf-iqliim bhi mil jaate
Hum ne to kuchh toote-phoote jumlon hii pe qanaat ki

Shohrat ke gahre dariya mein duube to phir ubhre nahin
Jin logon ko apna samjha jin logon se mohabbat ki

Eik doraaha aisa aaya donon toot ke gir jaate
Bachchon ke haathon ne sambhaala budhdhon hii ne hifaazat ki

Jaama-e-ulfat bunte aaye rishton ke dhaagon se hum
Umr ki qainchi kaat gayi ab kaahe ko itni mehnat ki

She Served in the House of One...

She served in the house of one, and loved the other with all her heart
She fulfilled both her duties, and spent her life in prayer

Had we prayed for more, the world would have been ours
Instead, we were content with just some broken words

Once they entered the river of fame, they never emerged,
Those we thought were our own, those whom we loved

At that fork in the road, we might both have fallen
Had our children not steadied us, had our elders not protected us

We wove the robe of love with the threads of relationships
The scissor of age has cut it to shreds; why did we work so hard?

Naqsh ki Tarah Ubharna Bhi…

Naqsh ki tarah ubharna bhi tumhi se seekha
Rafta rafta nazar aana bhi tumhi se seekha

Tum se haasil hua ik gahre samundar ka sukoot
Aur har mauj se ladna bhi tumhi se seekha

Achchhe sheron ki parakh tum ne hii sikhlaayi mujhe
Apne andaaz se kahna bhi tumhi se seekha

Tum ne samjhaaye miri soch ko aadaab adab
Lafz-o-maani se ulajhna bhi tumhi se seekha

Rishta-e-naaz ko jaana bhi to tum se jaana
Jaama-e-fakḥr pahanna bhi tumhi se seekha

Chhoti si baat pe ḳhush hona mujhe aata thha
Par badi baat pe chup rahna tumhi se seekha

To Emerge Like an Inscription...

How to emerge like an inscription, I learnt this from you
How to appear gradually into sight, this too I learnt from you

I gained from you the silence of a deep, vast ocean
How to fight each rising wave, this too I learnt from you

You taught me the skill to tell good verse from bad
How to say things in my own way, this too I learnt from you

You tutored me in the intricacies of the arts and etiquette
How to tangle with the meaning of words, this too I learnt from you

If at all I learnt the meaning of grace, it was from you
How to wear the robe of pride, this too I learnt from you

I knew how to be happy with small things
To be quiet about a big thing, I learnt this from you

Jo Dil Ne Kahii...

Jo dil ne kahii lab pe kahaan aai hai dekho
Ab mahfil-e-yaaraan mein bhi tanhaai hai dekho

Phoolon se hawa bhi kabhi ghabraai hai dekho
Ghunchon se bhi shabnam kabhi katraai hai dekho

Ab zauq-e-talab wajh-e-junoon thhair gaya hai
Aur arz-e-wafa baais-e-ruswai hai dekho

Gham apne hii ashkon ka ḳharidaar hua hai
Dil apni hi haalat ka tamashaai hai dekho

What the Heart Has Said...

What the heart has said hasn't come to the lips,
There is solitude even in this gathering of friends

Has the wind ever been nervous of flowers?
Has the dew ever evaded the blooms?

Now the pleasure of seeking has stayed the cause of madness
And the request for constancy is the cause of disgrace

Sorrow has become the buyer of its own tears
The heart is now the spectator of its own condition

Der Tak Raushni Rahi...

Der tak raushni rahi kal raat
Main ne odhi thhi chaandni kal raat

Eik muddat ke baad dhund chhatti
Dil ne apni kahi suni kal raat

Ungliyaan aasman chhuti thhiin
Haan miri dastaras mein thhi kal raat

Uthhta jaata thha parda-e-nisyaan
Eik eik baat yaad thhi kal raat

Taaq-e-dil pe thhi ghungruon ki sada
Eik jharhi sii lagi rahi kal raat

Jugnuon ke se lamhe urhte thhe
Meri mutthi mein aa gai kal raat

Light Lingered for a Long Time...

Light lingered for a long time last night
I draped myself in moonlight last night

The mist cleared after a long, long time
The heart spoke and heard itself last night

The fingers seemed to touch the sky
Yes, the night was within reach last night

The curtain of forgetfulness began to lift
Every little thing was remembered last night

Anklets echoed in the heart's niche
A ceaseless rain fell all night last night

Moments, like fireflies, flickered and flew about
I caught the night in my fist last night

Gardish-e-Mina-o-Jaam...

Gardish-e-mina-o-jaam dekhiye kab tak rahe
Hum pe taqaaza haraam dekhiye kab tak rahe

Tera sitam hum pe aam dekhiye kab tak rahe
Talḳhi-e-dauraan pe naam dekhiye kab tak rahe

Chhaa gaiin tareekiyan kho gaya husn-e-nazar
Waada-e-deedar-e-aam dekhiye kab tak rahe

Ahl-e-ḳhirad sust-rau ahl-e-junun tez-gaam
Shauq ka ye ehtimaam dekhiye kab tak rahe

Subh ke suraj ki zau dekhiye kab tak na aaye
Dahr pe ye rang-e-shaam dekhiye kab tak rahe

Let Us See How Long...

Let us see how long the goblets and glasses circulate
Let us see how long [the wine] will be forbidden to us

Let us see how long your tyranny will remain our lot
Let us see if your name survives the bitterness of this age

Darkness has spread, prudence is lost
Let us see how long the promise of a meeting remains

Men of wisdom are slow, the zealous are swift
Let us see how long the arrangements of passion will last

Let us see how long it takes for dawn to break
Let us see how long the afterglow lasts

Hamein To Aadat-e-Zakhm-e-Safar...

Humein to aadat-e-zaḳhm-e-safar hai kya kahiye
Yahan pe raah-e-wafa muḳhtasar hai kya kahiye

Judaiyan to ye maana badi qayaadat hain
Rafaqaton mein bhi dukh kis qadar hai kya kahiye

Hikayaat-e-ġham-e-duniya taveel thhi kah dii
Hikayaat-e-ġham-e-dil muḳhtasar hai kya kahiye

Majaal-e-deed nahin hasrat-e-nazaara sahi
Ye silsila hii bahut moatabar hai kya kahiye

We are Used to the Wounds...

We are used to the wounds of this journey
The path of fidelity here is short, what can we say?

Separations, we agree, can be a great guidance
There is such sorrow in friendships, what can we say?

The story of the world's sorrows was long, but we told it
The story of the heart's sorrows is short, what can we say?

If not the courage to behold, let there be the longing to see
This state of affairs is so trusted, what can we say?

Har Aan Sitam Dhaaye Hai...

Har aan sitam dhaaye hai kya jaaniye kya ho
Dil-e-ġham se bhi ghabraaye hai kya jaaniye kya ho

Kya ġhair ko dhundein ki tire kooche mein har eik
Apna sa nazar aaye hai kya jaaniye kya ho

Aankhon ko nahin raas kisi yaad ka aansu
Thham thham ke dhalak jaaye hai kya jaaniye kya ho

Isss bahr mein hum jaison pe har mauja-e-pur-ḳhoon
Aaa aa ke guzar jaaye hai kya jaaniye kya ho

Duniya se niraale hain tiri bazm ke dastoor
Jo aaye so pachhtaye hai kya jaaniye kya ho

Every Coy Gesture Inflicts Torture...

Every coy gesture inflicts torture, who knows what will be?
The heart is afraid of sorrow; who knows what will be?

Why look for the other? For in your lane everyone
Looks like one's own; who knows what will be?

The eyes don't like the tears of a certain recall
They roll down haltingly; who knows what will be?

For people like us, every blood-filled wave in this sea
Comes and goes; who knows what will be?

The ways of your gathering are unlike anything in this world
Whoever comes here repents; who knows what will be?

Hum Log Jo Khaak...

Hum log jo ḳhaak chhante hain
Mitti se guhar nikaalte hain

Hai shoala-e-deen ki sham-e-kufr
Parwaane kahan ye jaante hain

Isss gumbad-e-be-sada mein hum log
Alfaaz ke but taraashte hain

Ai saya-e-abr ab to ruk ja
Ik umr se dhoop katte hain

Those of Us Who Sift Through Dirt...

Those of us who sift through dirt
Bring out jewels from the earth

An ember of faith or candle of unbelief
What do the moths know of it?

In this dome of no sounds
We carve statues of words

O shadow of a cloud, stop for us now
We have been facing the sun for an eternity

Raunaqein Ab Bhi Kiwarhon...

Raunaqein ab bhi kiwarhon mein chhipi lagti hain
Mahfilein ab bhi issi tarah saji lagti hain

Raushni ab bhi darwaazon se umad aati hai
Khirkiyan ab bhi sadaaon si khuli lagti hain

Saa.atein jo teri qurbat mein giraan guzri theen
Duur se dekhoon to ab vo bhi bhali lagti hain

Ab bhi kuchh log sunaatey hain sunaaye hue sher
Baatein ab bhi teri zahnon mein basi lagti hain

Splendours Still Hide...

Splendours still seem to hide behind doors
Gatherings still seem as festive as before

Light still floods out of doors
Windows still open as if to calls

The hours spent with you that cost me so dear
Seen from this distance, they too seem good

Even now some people recite verses heard before
Even now only your words permeate every mind

Basti Mein Kuchh Log...

Basti mein kuchh log niraale ab bhi hain
Dekho ḳhaali daaman waale ab bhi hain

Dekho vo bhi hain jo sab kaḥ sakte thhe
Dekho un ke munh par taale ab bhi hain

Dekho un aankhon ko jinhon ne sab dekha
Dekho un par ḳhauf ke jaale ab bhi hain

Dekho ab bhi jins-e-wafa naayaab nahin
Apni jaan pe khelne waale ab bhi hain

Taare maand huwe par zarre raushan hain
Mitti mein aabaad ujaale ab bhi hain

There Are Still Some Rare People...

There are still some rare people left in this town
Look, there are still those with empty hands

Look, there are those who can say what must be said
Look, there are yet locks upon their lips

Look at those eyes that have seen everything
Look, there are still cobwebs of terror over them

Look, the wares of faithfulness are still not rare
Look, there are still those who will risk their lives

The stars have dimmed but the atoms are still bright
There is still radiant light alive in the dust

Ruk Ja Hujoom-e-Gul...

Ruk ja hujoom-e-gul ke abhi hausla nahin
Dil se ḳhayaal-e-tangi-e-daamaan gaya nahin

Jo kuchh hain sang-o-ḳhisht hain ya gard-e-rah-guzar
Tum tak jo aaye unn ka koi naqsh-e-paa nahin

Har aastaan pe likhkha hai ab naam-e-shahryar
Wabistagaan-e-dil ke liye koi jaa nahin

Sad-haif uss ke haath hai har zaḳhm ka rafu
Daaman mein jis ke eik bhi taar-e-wafa nahin

Stop! O Crowd of Flowers...

Stop! O crowd of flowers, for I don't have the courage yet,
The thought of my meagre means still lingers in my heart

Only stones and pebbles, or dust that hangs above the road;
Of those who came to you, no footprints can be seen

The king's name is written on each and every threshold
There's no one now left for the heart's attachment

Alas! His hands alone can stitch every wound—
He, who has no thread of constancy in his being

ACKNOWLEDGEMENTS

It is a truth much acknowledged in publishing circles, especially in India, that poetry is difficult to sell. And poetry in translation more so. Therefore, I am very grateful to Ravi Singh for not merely agreeing to publish this collection of Urdu poetry in translation but doing so with such whole-hearted enthusiasm. What is more, in all my years in writing and publishing books (32 years to be precise!), I have never had an editor who has been more invested, more engaged, more immersed in the making of a book. I must also thank Jerry Pinto for his close reading and suggestions.

Needless to say, I am also very grateful to Zehra Nigah, in the first instance, for granting permission and for trusting me with her work.

www.ingramcontent.com/pod-product-compliance
Lightning Source LLC
La Vergne TN
LVHW091158150826
845672LV00005B/1193